MW01598345

the *Holy* educated

MOTHERF*CKER

A FILTER-FREE GUIDE TO GETTING THROUGH THE UNTHINKABLE

dr. Nicole D. Price

the *Holy* educated

MOTHERF*CKER

A FILTER-FREE GUIDE TO GETTING THROUGH THE UNTHINKABLE

Josh, thanks for supporting me

dr. Nicole D. Price

Table of Contents

Foreward 1

1. Thirteen Seventy-Four   5

WHY THIS BOOK? 8

GUTTER BEHAVIOR 12

WHY THE TITLE? 14

2. Holy   19

HOLY 19

PURPOSE 29

WHOLLY 32

HOLEY 39

PASSION 41

HOLEY EXPERIENCES 43

3. Educated — 47

EDUMACATED 59

OPPORTUNITY 63

SMART 65

4. Motherf*cker — 69

BAD MOTHERF*CKERS 73

THIS MOTHERF*CKA! 76

MOTHERF*CKA PLEASE! 88

5. Operation 1374 — 94

THE HEMF SURVIVAL GUIDE 98

PRIVATE WORKSHOPS 116

FOOTNOTE REFERENCES 117

REFERENCES BY PAGE NUMBER 118

FOREWARD

WHAT DO YOU DO WHEN JOEL OSTEEN AND ARISTOTLE DON'T WORK?

– JIM "GRANDAD" NUNNELLY

"Who organized this event?"

It was a question I asked when I first met Dr. Nicole Price. She had lazily offered her time as a volunteer to a community event but I could tell that this time, the event had a highly technical brain involved. It's interesting to me that she doesn't always talk about her engineering degree. In fact it is something I am regularly trying to get her to change because there are three distinct disciplines that cause people to honor the work required to practice them - doctor, lawyer, and engineer. Who hides that they are an engineer? Well, Dr. Nicole Price doesn't always intend to hide it but this fact about her educational pursuits is typically an afterthought or late mention. I've come to see why. She undervalues its importance but not because it wasn't a huge accomplishment. She downplays it because she is a walking example of inclusion. Mostly because she didn't always have privilege, she truly wants everyone to be valued regardless of their educational background and accomplishments. In fact, for as long as I have known her, she has never once asked me what I do. The information has simply unfolded as part of our regular conversations with each other.

The greats are only held in such high regard because we have some insight into what they have overcome. They at least give us the impression that we know them. We get excited about Cardi B because she has worked as a stripper. She is not as impressive if her story starts out on the shores of West Kennebunk, Maine with parents who are multi millionaires. If fact, I'm not so certain that she could entertain and connect with as many people as she does if she had that storyline in her history. It is the "gutter behavior" that people align to. Interestingly enough, people who

1

have danced provocatively for money often keep their past a secret and try to hide that part of themselves from their new world. It's understandable considering one of the many complaints about Cardi B is that she was a stripper although that fact is directly tied to the current way she is free to artistically express herself through her words and also, more literally, how she dances on the stage.

Like all of us, there are lots of events that inform how Dr. Price shows up to the world each day. She hasn't always offered up the details. I was the first to ask her what she was hiding. I recall her being taken aback by the question. I have watched her be shocked time and time again when someone is surprised about some part of her storied past. She hasn't thought she was interesting enough to talk about her past. When reading this book, I couldn't disagree more. When she invited me to write the foreword, I first asked myself, "Why me?" I'm still not sure I have come to an answer. And that makes me a bit nervous because my job is to try to convince you to delve deeply into the life of someone, that unlike me, you likely don't know. To this point all you have is that she boldly put this provocative title before us. I finally came to the conclusion, that the reason I was asked doesn't matter as much as why I believe you should read this book.

Warning: don't let the title of this "search yourself" masterpiece fool you. While provocative, it helps to break it down word by word. "Holy" certainly describes the steeply religious and faith-filled life of Dr. Price. But what becomes clear is that it's hard to categorize her as a religious freak. She examines her own Christian upbringing in a way that seems boastful of her beliefs. Yet, she manages to give us unobstructed access to her faith without invoking any obligatory feelings to accept or adopt her faith principles. That alone makes this book unique. You can hardly find a book written by a Christian that doesn't have some call to discipleship. Frequently while reading about the "holy" aspect of her life, I was reminded of Shakespeare's famous quote, "To thine own self, be true." With that one phrase, he invited us to accept every part of our life as it is. In a Shakespearean sort of way, Price uses the "holy" content, not to convert, but to invite. She invites us to view the totality of our experiences as essential ingredients to the recipe of our lives. We are all created differently, especially as it relates to our faith and how we classify our experiences. That is not a novel idea. However, Dr. Price manages to uplift this idea with an ease and a grace that I greatly appreciate. In fact, she is so truthful about her experience, that I began to examine my own faith and how it has shaped me. This section definitely made me go, "Hmmmmm."

Further breaking down the title, "Educated" seems at first self-evident. However, you are challenged to understand and accept a widened view of "education." Dr. Price examined the need for us to see and appreciate the less universally accepted forms of education. As she treats the reader to an entertaining account of how she and her best friend chose what university to attend, my assertion that she was hiding something was put to rest. In this one passage, I saw just how far this sister is willing to go to expose who and what she is - even at the expense of appearing foolish. This section also challenged me to think about judging people based on their educational pursuits. It reinforced my strong belief that sometimes the most unconventional and overlooked people might be our best educators.

Last but not least is the "Motherf*cker" part of the book. Here she begins to tie up and explain why she uses this specific choice of words, especially as a title. Obviously, it has shock value. However, there's much more here than the blatant use of one of the most unacceptable words in the English language. In fact, she goes to great length to explain the variations in the use of this societal "no-no" term. She poignantly points out that this expression has varied meanings depending on how it is used. But, make no mistake, this section is as much a part of Dr. Nicole Price as the "Holy" and "Educated" parts. She insists that there is likely a mother*cker part in you, too.

Now if you're wondering about Price's main point for writing this book, you are not alone. It is a question I asked when she first gave me the manuscript. I know her as a chemical engineer, a leadership expert, and as an author of content related to diversity and inclusion. In fact, I wasn't quite sure why this book wasn't about one of those business topics. At one point, I even tried to get her to change it to make it more of a business book. In part, I wondered what her existing clients in various industries would think of the personal, transparent nature of the book and why they would invest in a session about a Holy Educated Motherf*cker. As I kept reading, it was clear to me that this book was not for businesses. It is for individuals like you. Oftentimes we are going through some really tough stuff. Dr. Price has decided to write about us, and for once, not about our jobs. Why? Because we are all more complicated than we let on and we have a wide range of experiences. However, interestingly enough, she still manages to slyly show us that we are not free from destructive blindness no matter how faith-filled or educated we might be. We are full of it and, by admitting that, in many ways she is full of it, too. She beckons us to confess the same.

I am over seventy-years old and yet I still believe The Holy Educated Motherf*cker provides the type of Cardi B transparency that makes us all more relatable. Dr. Price and I are not the same but we think alike. We both believe that first impressions should not be last impressions. Like her, I stand by the idea that one part of a person's story is at best an incomplete story. It takes all the ingredients to make the whole. We are not all educated saints. In fact most of us are not. Those things we try to hide? This book invites you to unleash a level of transparency admitting to and speaking about the never-talk-about-it situations in our lives. She challenges us to attack those things that Joel Osteen nor Aristotle would likely – the ones that make you go, "Did I do that?" What do you do when being holy and educated fail you? Dr. Price suggests that when we come face-to-face with these "gutter" moments, often our reaction is to try to hide them. That is not the way. She has done us all a good service by uncovering and sharing a few of her encounters. In The Holy Educated Motherf*cker she has set the example by starting first.

chapter one

thirteen
seventy-four

On January 26, 2001, I got paid. There was nothing unique about this payday. At the time, I was working as a chemical engineer for a private corporation which manufactured almost all of its products internally. I was paid fairly well and I was grateful but couldn't have been more neutral about the day. Only two years removed from college, I didn't have any student loans because I had secured a full academic scholarship. Additionally, because of a freak accident involving my dad, I had access to funds that were set aside for college and largely were left unused. I hadn't used that specific college fund money because each summer during college, I also worked as an intern for a pharmaceutical company making enough money to sustain my frugal lifestyle for almost the entire school year. Furthermore, I was sitting on a decent 401K because the company shared sizable profits at more than 10% for the first two years I had been working there. I felt I was lucky. Life was financially going pretty well for a twenty-something straight from the hood.

So why do I mention payday?

Because a little over one week later everything changed.

In 2001, I paid my daycare bill in cash weekly. First of all, it wasn't that expensive. Secondly, I paid for most things in cash back then. I was raised by people who moved in cash. For them, credit was for people who lived beyond their means. This isn't a financial book so I don't intend to drag out the merits and issues with that perspective. It is simply insight into why I went to the ATM to get some extra money to cover the daycare fee.

I pressed the buttons to withdraw $100. The screen said insufficient funds. I didn't worry because, in my mind, this had to be a mistake. I tried a lower dollar amount. I got the same error message so I then tried withdrawing the lowest dollar amount possible—$20. This darn ATM display read the same thing – insufficient funds. Confused, I conducted an inquiry to see how much money I had and that's when I saw that horrific number on the screen—$13.74.

That was my checking account balance. My savings account was worse, sitting solidly at zero dollars. Me? I was baffled. I lived below my means. I worked all the time. I did not engage in excess. I was so confused, my mind was racing. Was this some strange identity theft issue? Had the bank made a huge mistake? Had my then-husband been kidnapped by a drug cartel and required to pay a ransom to be freed? Regardless of what was going on in my head, I had to get to work. Remember, it's 2001 and years before my bank would have mobile banking options so I couldn't figure it out in the moment. In fact, I really couldn't figure it out when I got to work either. While I had internet access at work at the time, it wasn't all-access use. The internet was for research purposes only[1]. In order to access my bank account information, I would have to go to the physical bank. My options were to wait until lunchtime to inquire about this or call in so I could go to the bank immediately when it opened. I'm not the kind of person to call in for hardly anything and whatever caused this unthinkable situation for me, it could wait until after I got to work to be resolved.

If you knew me well, you'd know that I never get to work early, though. I arrive just about five minutes before I am expected. At the time, the first shift standup meeting was at 7:30AM and the project engineer was expected to be there. And I still had to drop off my baby. In haste, I called my mother and told her I didn't know what happened but that I needed the money for daycare. She took care of it, I dropped my child off, and got to work by my usual 7:24AM. A question I receive often is, "How did you continue with your day?" The answer is honestly that I do not know. When I think back on it the only explanation I have is that I was not culturally raised to allow external influences to get in the way of my commitments and my goals.

Over the course of the next few weeks, I learned that none of what I was hypothesizing about my money's disappearance

---

[1] If we ever meet in person, remind me to tell you about the time I searched "do-it" on my work computer.

was true. I also learned that what was true was that I had hardly any liquid cash and almost all my bills were behind, including utilities[2]. Worst of all, unbeknownst to me, even my corporate card had been used for non-business expenses. I had new debts that I didn't know anything about, I wasn't getting paid for three more weeks, my mortgage was due, and every Monday I would need to have that daycare money if I planned to go to the production plant without a kid on my hip[3].

WHY THIS BOOK?

What is filter-free really? I don't want you to think this book is a tell-all memoir. It is not. I honestly don't think I am interesting enough. Rather, this book is an unbridled account of the strategies I have used to overcome a long list of unthinkables. The filter-free designation was birthed from a time when I worked in Human Resources. HR professionals, if I use sweeping generalizations, are the kind of personalities that can think some of the most brutal things about people. Yet, when they open their mouths to speak something comes out that sounds like a small pebble landing on a pillow. They are tactful. They seem to care a great deal about how what they say will impact the listener. On the other hand, I tend to value truth a little more than I value tact. However, if I were to conduct a self-assessment, I am not a person with loose lips who says whatever I want to whomever I want, whenever I desire – my words are running through a filter. In fact, it is a six-layer, internal filter that asks;

1. Is it funny?

2. Is it true?

3. Is it in alignment with my purpose?

[2] Utilities? That really chaps my hide because I had previously set utilities up on autopay so an irrational indignation overcame me about those utility bills.

[3] I did it once. It's not allowed by the way.

4. Does it provoke thought?

5. Do I feel it needs to be said to push us forward?

6. Will I be free from regret afterwards?

Asking this series of six questions is a natural process for me. It is lightning fast and if the answers are yes, I am going to make the point. I am not literally filter-free because I do think about everything I say. But when you compare what I still manage to verbalize next to what most people are willing to say aloud, it appears to be filter-free.

When I worked in HR departments I learned to censor myself in a way that was unnatural for me because I was regularly hurting my colleagues' feelings when I didn't intend to. The level of censoring that included a 7th question, "Will anyone be hurt by this statement?" was draining for me. Consequently, each week by Friday I would be exhausted. In my exhaustion, I was uninterested in the 7th question and Fridays in the office became known as Filter-Free Friday. Literally, on Fridays, people would seek me out to determine what my position really was about an issue or a project. In contrast, the conversation was less about me blowing off steam but more about me openly sharing what needed to be said in order to make our company better. At times, that meant that some people's feelings would be hurt.

This is not a business book either though. I am not writing it to make companies better. This book represents my best attempt at sharing my life's greatest pains in order for other people to possibly find comfort in knowing that they are not alone when the unthinkable things happen. I am writing this book because I have healed, overcome my share of the unthinkables and I have done so while showing up for work in powerfully engaged ways. I think there is something to learn from that and from other parts of my path as well. As such, this book is a filter-free compilation of my personal learnings.

9

"Mistakes are a fact of life.

It is the response to the error that counts."

- NIKKI GIOVANNI

Prior to now, there were less than a handful of living, breathing people who knew the particulars of the 1374 story and many of the others that you will read about in this book. While I am an open person, I do not make a habit of historical storytelling especially in written form. I typically prefer to revel in what can be in the future rather than what was done in the past. Regardless, the benefits of my sharing these tidbits far outweigh the pain I am sure to feel as people I know and even some I don't know, judge my journey through their lenses. The learnings from the past, the beauty of the present and the hopes for the future are the only things that make living worth the effort and that is why this book.

No matter your unthinkable situation, it is yours. Once there, faced with the unthinkable, it is not helpful to wish for something different. If by chance, we have the ability to shift the course of history, then being faced with the unthinkable loses its sting. Whether at your own doing, the doing of some other person or group or by unfortunate stroke of luck, when we are face to face with something we never thought possible, there is always something we do have the ability to do—choose how to craft our response.

Thirteen seventy-four and the other stories in this book are stories of overcoming the unthinkable. I have written this book because I know that although I made a stupid decision or two, those decisions did not represent my destruction. God gave me rams in the bushes, not singular, but plural. God also gave me a testimony about grit, empathy, compassion and something that I am not sure everyone will be able to get their heads around – gutter behavior.

GUTTER BEHAVIOR

Allow me tell you a story about Oma Dell Price, my paternal grandmother. When I was young, I was an incredibly judgmental, high-saddity, snobby young person. Whenever I would talk to my grandmother about something that someone did that I perceived to be morally wrong, I would usually be livid and express how I just couldn't believe how someone could do this thing or that thing. Her response was always patient, kind and simple; keep living baby.

> ## "Keep living, baby."
>
> - OMA DELL PRICE

Based on my lived experience, my granny was right. She was right about the fact that as I have lived longer and experienced more, I understand first-hand, how well-meaning people can make stupid decisions. These decisions sometimes work out, other times they impact the deciding party negatively. Conversely, well-meaning people can also decide to do things that impact other people in hurtful and destructive ways, too. Neither is a reason to give up or to sit it out. When you mess up, fix it as best you can. When you end up in an unthinkable situation, it will probably feel unfair. It is likely that you weren't ready for it because by definition, you didn't expect or think you would be faced with this challenge. But one thing I know for sure is that all of us, if we have lived long enough, have faced the unthinkable. We have been on the receiving end, getting the short end of some kind of proverbial stick. In contrast, we have also messed up and over someone, somewhere along the way, causing unthinkable situations for someone else. None of us are without a bone in a closet or some gutter behavior here or there.

I know this for sure. Yet, I don't think that reality is a reason for you to emotionally stay down in the dumps. I may not have had the same experiences as you, but I have had my share of unthinkable events. My ability to pivot is better than average but I have not always been above deep emotional, depressive dumps as a result of experiencing the unthinkable. If you too, have been in the dumps before, are currently feeling a bit downtrodden or just haven't lived long enough to experience either, you are the reason I have written this book. It is a common experience and when faced with it, we all need some strategies for how to get out or just a little motivation.

This book is designed to motivate anyone who has ever found themselves in a precarious place and have been faced with the unthinkable. It is for those of you who have made "stupid" choices and need to forgive yourself and others. It is for anyone struggling with accepting themselves in the aftermath. I am writing it to demonstrate how the worst of unthinkable situations can create the best opportunities if you look for them. In this book, I strive to uplift the human spirit but with a huge caveat. I hope to do so without engaging in spiritual malpractice. It is often an outcome of many books that invite people to shift from victims to victors via an intense focus on inner peace. I do not intend to overly focus on this path toward an internally peaceful state. While I do believe inner peace is important and vital, I also believe that truly peaceful people are the ones who are actually capable of inflicting great harm to other people and possibly capable of immense despair. I imagine that if you are not capable of causing great harm to yourself or others then you are actually just harmless, not necessarily peaceful. The peaceful person is the one who chooses peace instead of resorting to harm, great violence or incredible despair when his or her back is against the wall.

Anger and despair are real emotional responses to unthinkable events. They can also spark people into action even if they are not ideal steady-state emotions. Most self-help books try to push people to skip past anger and despair, sometimes offering

13

advice that actually diminishes who people are inherently rather than honoring and lifting them up. These are complaints I have and I hope not to perpetuate. I hope to uplift you and help you find your own way forward by learning from the "dumps" of my journey. Self-reflection is critical but not in the way you think. Overcoming the unthinkable is not about dissecting every wrong turn you've made. It is more about reflecting on how those wrong turns and all of your experiences really can be used to help you find your way out today and in the future. This is a fine line because it can't be done without looking at yourself and the totality of your experiences. It is a fine line that can be toed and I will attempt to toe that line in this offering to you.

WHY THE TITLE?

I, like many people, have a complicated relationship with some of my family members. If I were to simplify the challenges, the complications started from the moment I started talking because of my personality traits. I have six siblings and I am the only one who is extroverted and I am a very clear extrovert. Both my parents were introverts too so I was surrounded by introverts. From the start, just my mere talking was an issue. In fact, one of the first items I remember receiving when I was a kid was a plaque that said, "Dear Lord help me this day to keep my big mouth shut."

I was a talker.

In all that talking, I also wasn't shy about sharing my opinions and ideas about innumerable topics especially my perception of apparent injustices. I have noticed that adults who highlight injustices are not popular. In fact, many of them have their lives ended early because people do not appreciate the ways in which they upset the status quo. Speaking up isn't always valued in adults and it certainly isn't a valued characteristic in children. This is especially true when your birth order is sixth. The sixth child is considered one of the "babies" in the family. The translation is that there are a plethora of people telling you what to do and not listening to you tell them how things should be done.

Nonetheless, whenever I would get on my soapbox about issues, yep you guessed it, I was called a "holy, educated motherf*cker." I hated it and did not view it as a term of endearment. In fact, I am certain that it was everything but a term of endearment. It was a name that often got under my thin skin faster than a New York minute. If you wanted to rile me up, call me something other than Nicole[4]. If you wanted to start a physical fight, call me "little 'holy, educated, motherf*cker.'" Everyone knows when "little" is used as an adjective it is by and large used to belittle. To add insult to injury, "holy, educated motherf*cker" was always preceded with "you little..."

The nickname was intended to sting and intended to single out. Worse, it was suggesting that I singled myself out. That's significant because isolating—singling someone out—creates discomfort, and nobody likes to be alone or uncomfortable. We are a social species. We grow, learn, work and evolve together. So to accuse someone of choosing to separate from the group is a major breach of typical social contracts. And there's no way to defend against it. If you're too vocal in defense of yourself, then the allegation must be true because otherwise why would you be so defensive. If you're silent and don't refute it at all, well then it's certainly true because why wouldn't you refute it. I would vacillate between the two defensive extremes, never finding a place that felt comfortable. Even with all of that history, I was never so irritated as when my niece used the "holy, educated motherf*cker" adage.

My great niece had gotten into a fight[5] at school and my niece proudly posted a video of the melee on social media. In a private message, I asked her mother, my niece, to take the post down for fear that the error in judgment would result in future challenges for my great niece when it was time for her to go to college. My niece has since vehemently apologized but at the time she was

---

[4] Darling Nikki was especially irritating for me. Thanks Prince.

[5] Having very few de-escalation strategies, she mollywhops people all the time.

furious with me and posted a very public and direct quote[6], "...
Oh she's not gonna get accepted in college..WHERE THE F*CK
was u holy, educated ass Muthaf*ckas YEARS AGO??? Huh?..."

I was hurt but it was one of the best things that could have ever
happened to me as evidenced by what happened next. Ruminating
over her words and playing the statement over and over again
in my mind, I fell asleep and had a vivid, seemingly unrelated
dream about competing in a tug of war competition. God speaks
to me in my dreams[7]. Consequently, the morning after, while
interpreting my own dream, it became clear to me that I am all
three things. I am holy. I am educated. And as much as I hate to
admit it, I am a motherf*cker. I had been fighting the label for
as long as I could remember. I was battling with people I loved,
tugging on a rope of respectability when there was no disrespect
if I just owned it. Through this experience, God showed me that
there are two ways to get yourself out of a tug of war battle – pull
harder or let go of the rope. I chose my method, let go of the
rope and accepted the name. In fact, I did more than accept the
name, I embraced it. I am a holy, educated, motherf*cker. I just
simply don't want to use my energy to "pull harder" trying to
convince people I am something different. It hadn't worked in all
these years and maybe it hadn't worked because it is who I am.

The other thing I've come to believe is that I am not the only
holy, educated, motherf*cker. There are other people who feel they
also don't fit the norms of typical descriptions and those people
have been faced with the unthinkable too. Just as the normal
approaches haven't been the best for them in general either, their
way out of the unthinkable has likely been unconventional as
well. Everyone, when faced with the unthinkable could use some
motivation and a smidge of self-acceptance. But for people who

---

[6] Ouch! Insert licked wounds here.

[7] Not in a "God told me to tell you" kind of way. I use the Virkler method which is
only about what God is saying to you about you.

"… Oh she's not gonna get accepted into college... WHERE THE F*CK was u holy, educated ass Muthaf*ckas YEARS AGO??? Huh?..."

- MY NIECE

feel left out and left behind in any way, I believe it is definitely a requirement if you are going to overcome the unthinkable. When all is well, you might not need this book. When you are in the gutter, people will fail you and you might be scrambling to find support. That is when you will need some unorthodox strategies.

The public dragging on social media was my encounter. The tussling match between the holy, educated and motherf*cker parts of me was over and that was the genesis of all my worlds coming together. So let this be your encounter. You've already picked up a book with motherf*cker in the title; I think it's safe to say you're open to possibilities. Maybe you're even looking for your watershed moment. I'm here to tell you, you can be more than you thought— different than you imagined. If the observers call you odd, it's time to embrace it. Perhaps you are in an unthinkable place right this moment. You may not believe it but your oddness and the challenge of the moment are where your power lies. Power not strength. If strength were all, the tiger would not fear the scorpion. Your odd personality, your experiences (even the unthinkable ones), and your ability to be guttural are all sources of power for you if you look for it. It is my hope that this book will assist you on your journey of discovery. This filter-free book is for you, well, and for me. Hi, my name is Dr. Nicole D. Price, and I'm a holy, educated motherf*cker.

chapter two

To date, there has only been one time that I felt separated from God. During that time, when I prayed, it felt like I might as well have been talking to a brick wall. If Gospel music started to play, it was emotionally overwhelming and I would turn it off. I would sit in sanctuaries unable to stomach any pomp and circumstance. As an example, if there was a requirement to stand when the minister walked in, I would do it but I was frustrated. Opening statements that were the same, rote, memorized and repeated so quickly that no unfamiliar person would know what was being said, made my skin crawl. My frustration mostly stemmed from the emptiness I was feeling. The rituals seemed disconnected from what I needed in the moment. However, my feelings were exacerbated by the inkling I had that if I mentioned that I was feeling empty and disconnected from God, I thought I knew what my spiritual leaders would offer as advice.

> God is always
> there for you.
>
> God will never leave
> you nor forsake you.

I had said these things to other people. But what had I really been through when I was offering that advice? For me, in previous situations, this advice was all coming from surface-level, academic or theological understanding, not the deep, spiritual, soul connection that I hadn't yet lived through but needed during this time.

What's interesting is that unlike many people who feel separated from God, I wasn't confused at all about how the spiritual disconnection happened. I knew exactly when and how I ended up in this space. My mama was killed by a drunk driver and I was the only one lucid enough to manage the business of dealing with her death and the requirements associated with our family instantly becoming victims in a murder trial. It was time for me to be the holy, educated, motherf*cker and I'm not sure I leaned into it perfectly. What I did instead was push down every emotion and tap into this do-what-you-got-to-do mentality. In that suppression, I went too far. I had cut off almost all emotions. When you cut off negative feelings in order to protect yourself or to keep moving, one consequence is that you also cut off positive feelings like connectedness to God and even connectedness to people as well. That was my state of mind when I personally met Byron Katie.

In 2014, when I agreed to attend her nine-day workshop at the School for The Work conference in Ojai, California, I was in some ways working. Meaning I was there to professionally learn about how to help people take personal accountability for their actions. It was my job to be there to learn about that topic. However, in the most important way, I was there to see if, by chance, the lady who said she was crazy and then God spoke to her through cockroaches[8] had something to offer that would help.

There were hundreds of people at the School for the Work but not everyone attended everything. Morning activities had fewer people than the evening events but I attended all the sessions and followed the instructions as given. It was in a very full evening session activity when Byron Katie asked the religious people to stand up. For me, at the time, religious and spiritual meant the same thing. In a lot of ways, they still do. After all, I don't understand why anyone would engage in religious fanfare without the spiritual connection. Conversely, regularly engaging in a spiritual practice is the definition of religious ritual. Regardless, I didn't realize at the time that she was making a very keen delineation. Clearly, almost all of the participants made that same distinction as well.

---

[8] I've yet to hear the voice of God through cockroaches but eh.

21

When I stood up, I was shocked to see that there were only about four other people who stood up with me. My shock was because this was a conference where we spent the mornings doing meditative walks, meditated before the morning session, and willfully spent an entire day in silence to connect with God. In my mind, what was this if not the actions of religious people? Later that evening, some of the participants demonstrated what they thought the difference was between religious (i.e. me) and spiritual (i.e. them). During that exercise, I learned that hundreds of people at this conference viewed religious people as folks who are intolerant, loud, mean and nasty towards other people. These spiritual people were asked to play out stereotypes of religious people. They were screaming obscenities like "God hates f*gs" and "Baby killer" and "Turn your life around or you are going to hell." I was mortified. I didn't believe or behave in any of those ways but I am religious. They associated religious people with obnoxious signage, in-your-face evangelism and largely something other than what I professed myself to be—a permission evangelist.

In all, it was a great exercise. It showed me how I, too, judge people based on labels. The exercise highlighted the ways that I may have shared my broader beliefs with others when it wasn't timely, necessary or helpful[9]. I cannot deny that those people opened my eyes to the vast ways that people have been hurt under the auspice of being holy. After all, people in the church have hurt me. However, I maintain that I am not merely spiritual, even by their definition. I go to church almost every Sunday. I read my Bible. I pray about everything from not getting a speeding ticket to world peace. While I do not own the hate associated with the rituals, I perform the rituals. I am religious. More specifically, I am Christian.

I was born into the Christian faith. I say "born" because I don't remember when I wasn't a Christian. My parents were

---

[9] I guess my family was right about all that talking. I work on it constantly.

Christian and their parents were Christian. From as long as I could recall, I prayed to Jesus, studied the scriptures in the Bible, and went to church every Sunday. When I left home to go to college, I had missed exactly one Sunday attending church.

I had the chickenpox.

Otherwise, I was generally at my church, in worship with someone, somewhere or learning about Jesus two to four days each week. When I was baptized at eight or nine years old, it stands out because by then it was just a symbol of what I believed in my heart which was that Jesus was the author and finisher of my faith[10]. Before I left grammar school, I had seen everyone I love associate Jesus with overcoming the unthinkable and with salvation. I believed it so much that when I got the courage to go up to the front of the sanctuary to profess Jesus Christ as my personal Lord and Savior, the only reason I needed courage was my hair. Yep, my hair.

Every Saturday my mother would spend hours getting my afro straightened. Any moisture and it was reverting back to this kinky ball that naturally grew towards the sky. For some reason that I did not understand, on Sundays it needed to have been blown dry to look more like a weeping willow tree and then pressed with a hot comb until it was bone straight. This process took forever and kept me from my beloved Saturdays. More than anything, because I'm tender headed, it was painful.

This Sunday, after the arduous Saturday hair frying ordeal, I walked down the aisle, hair sleek, resting neatly on my shoulders, and before hundreds of witnesses, I said I wanted to be Christian formally. Everyone was thrilled. I think my mother was concerned a wee bit about her Saturday labor but she tried to act like it wasn't an issue. Later that evening I was baptized in really cold water to the hum of I Know It

---

[10] I thought I'd add a little Missionary Baptist jargon for emphasis.

23

I know it
was the blood.
I know it
was the blood.
I know it was the
blood for me.

One day when I was
lost, he died upon
the cross. I know it
was the blood for me.

- EVELYN SIMPSON-CURENTON

Was the Blood. The lyrics are still among my favorites.

My hair did not make it, though. Immediately before my big dip, my mama attempted to wrap my hair around my head and put a swim cap on me. I could tell the cap wasn't working as intended before I even walked down to the basement of the church where the baptismal pool was located. My hair had already started reverting earlier in the day because of ambient moisture from humidity and sweat. It hadn't reverted all the way back but it was starting to resemble the familiar willow tree. As such, you just can't brush a "willow tree" under a swim cap. I was so focused on my first communion and equally excited about getting my own special bible with my name and baptism date in it, that I don't recall what my hair looked like afterward. I couldn't have cared any less.

What I do remember is that before my baptism I was at church a lot but regularly caught the church bus, which operated only on Sundays. From baptism forward, I was at the church every time the door opened. At one point, my mama even had keys. I was all in. By middle school I was proud to be the reigning champion, memorizing all 100 of the most popular scriptures. By my senior year in high school, I was winning every extemporaneous biblical topic speaking competition in the Union District Congress in Missouri. In fact, one of my favorite things to do on Wednesday nights at Bible study was to debate my pastor on issues of discrimination. Engaging in formal religious rituals and activities was my life and it started early.

When I was in second grade, I met my first friend of a different religion. Her name was Khalilah and she was delightful. Like almost all my friends still to date, Khalilah was quite introverted. Our friendship was mostly one of general play and me talking while she listened. She rarely spoke unless I asked her a direct question.

Khalilah was a Muslim and she invited me to attend the mosque with her. I have no idea what my dad would have thought of that because he was in the hospital recovering from injuries but my mama said yes. I don't recall the details of my experience but I do remember all the women had their hair covered and I was shocked

25

seeing Black women like this. When I attended my church some people wore hats but again, most of us had spent the entire day on Saturday getting our hair ready for church on Sunday morning. There wasn't any way I would cover my hair after all that straightening but it looked like they all had straight hair under their hijabs. In all, my experience was good and the women were incredibly nice and warm. So as any good friend would do, I invited Khalilah to my church.

Khalilah always wore a hijab so it was pretty obvious to ascertain that she wasn't Christian. What was more apparent was that other people could tell Khalilah wasn't Christian, thought that was an issue, felt they needed to do something about it, and set about with a sort of passive aggressive recruitment strategy. During Sunday school and worship, there were far more mentions of Jesus being the only way to salvation than I ever remembered from any of my other prior visits to church. It was stated with enough plainness, precision and emphasis that anyone like Khalilah was doomed to hell if she didn't deny Allah and profess Jesus that my young brain understood it clearly. I was mortified and watching that experience still informs the way I think about Christianity today. I feel like my job is to help Christians be more accepting of people of different faiths.

Well-meaning people approach organized religion because they need something. I find this to be especially true when people who weren't raised to practice a particular faith show up in a church, temple, mosque, etc. The last thing they expect is to be othered[11]. A motivation behind singling people out is to make everybody fall in line. However, visitors in our religious dwellings are our guests and expect to be treated as such. Although I didn't know the word at the time, my friend was being othered and I didn't like it one bit so I set out on a personal journey to study the similarities between Islam and Christianity and not because I was a scholar. I did it because Khalilah and I had one major thing in common, we were friends so certainly our religions had to be similar. Right?

[11] No one is coming to church to be treated poorly.

26

The only resource I had available to me at the time was our family's set of the Encyclopedia Britannica. If you aren't familiar, before the internet if you could not get to the library, many people had the "library" at home. A point of personal pride for me was that, for all we did not have, our family had a complete set of books, arranged alphabetically that offered information on many subjects including Islam – the encyclopedia. At the time I was a poor reader so I needed lots of help. The problem was that there was no way any one person in the house was going to be patient enough to sit with me for as long as I needed. So I solicited the help of anyone who would assist me in short stints until I had the information I was seeking.

The first thing I learned in the encyclopedia was that Allah is not a different God but that Allah is God in Arabic. Knowing that the word was merely a translation issue was all I needed but I kept studying so that I could be a good friend to Khalilah. As a second grader, I believed that if God demanded anything of me in that moment, God wanted me to be a good friend. In my study, I also learned that in Islam and Christianity followers believe that there is only one God. Both religions use a holy book considered to be the word of God; the Bible and the Quran. Both have a creation story in which God created the universe from nothing. The ethical teachings of both religions are almost indistinguishable—faith, compassion, love, justice and discipline. In recent history, there have been many social experiments where a researcher would read a passage from the Quran or Bible and try to get people to guess which book the passage was from only to have most people fail. People, especially Christians, don't really know the difference. Besides, both in Christianity and Islam followers believe that God sent prophets to spread the word of God and that Abraham was the father of those beliefs, which is why they are both called Abrahamic religions. At seven, I began to believe that Khalilah's parents were her prophets just as much as, if not more than, my parents were my prophets. As such, I fully believe that had I been born to her parents and she to mine, she would be Christian and I would be Muslim. We remained friends until I changed schools.

I consider myself to be holy. Yet, I am not surprised when people are shocked that I am Christian. After all, while I believe in the

Ho·ly

/ 'hōlē /

adjective

dedicated or consecrated to God
or a religious purpose; sacred.

death, burial and resurrection of Jesus Christ, I believe that it is illogical to believe that every, single, solitary person who doesn't believe that theology is going to hell and conversely that every, single, solitary person who has done no more than profess that belief is going to heaven. I refuse to argue with people about it because faith is not factual. Faith is a belief. My belief has helped me through many unthinkable situations and that has been more than good enough for me. I am not threatened to learn about other religions because I have no intention of changing my faith and don't expect to change anyone else's beliefs. There are enough people hurting and searching who don't follow any organized religion. There are so many people in that group that I don't feel obligated to attempt to convert people from other faiths to Christianity.

Furthermore, people don't think I am Christian because I also support many things that other Christians do not, such as I use words like motherf*cker. To me, being holy means something larger than cursing or not. Holy, by definition, means to be dedicated or consecrated to God. I am that. It also means to be dedicated or consecrated to a religious purpose. I am definitely that. I believe that I was created for a unique purpose and I am dedicated to that purpose. I also believe that other people are dedicated to at least one purpose, too. For me, all people who are dedicated to their purpose are holy – in some way and purpose is directly tied to work.

If you pay close attention to little children, they start out wanting to be helpful and to work. They desire to have some purpose in the world. They want to help you sweep and pour things. Too often, adults will hinder that interest because kiddos won't get up all the dirt when they sweep or they might spill a little when they attempt to pour drinks. However, we were born with a purpose to work. As such, it's a precarious thing for me when adults profess that teenagers and young adults are lazy. I see it differently, teenagers are not lazy. Teenagers are simply older toddlers who adults discouraged from working for years and then abruptly changed the rules. It is better to encourage and embrace children's willingness to work from the beginning of their lives rather than shooting them down. My guess is that if we tried that approach, children wouldn't resist chores and work as teens or young adults. Rather they would embrace making a contribution to the world through work and having a sense of shared purpose. The benefit for our children is that many people are drawn to their passions when they are quite young. Purpose-identification work often begins with the question, "What have you always liked to do?" In all the years I've assisted people with purpose-identification, I have never had a person earnestly say that sitting down and shutting up was meaningful to them. We have to stop starting children off in that way, telling them to sit down and shut up, if we want to see a more involved and engaged world. However, regardless of how the adults in your life approached this topic, you are never too young or old to figure out what the purpose of your life or work will be and that knowledge is critical to sticking it out when the unthinkable occurs.

PURPOSE

To identify your purpose, it is important to reflect on what you love to do, where you like to do it and with whom you like to do it. Sometimes people end up doing things because they were good at performing certain tasks or because the work was convenient or necessary. I am pretty clear that my purpose isn't to be an engineer but I studied it because it was convenient. I had a full scholarship. That doesn't mean that being an engineer wasn't part of my purposeful path. It also doesn't mean that I wasted my time in engineering school[12]. What is more true is that engineering school taught me several things that obtaining another degree wouldn't have and those perspectives indirectly inform many of the things I do today. What you're currently doing may not be your ultimate purpose but whatever it is, it is part of your purposeful path. For many people, purpose is hard to identify at times because, when a person is aligned to their "purpose work," the work can seem effortless and sometimes, not that important. Skill, talent and abilities that come easiest to us can sometimes be taken for granted and overlooked. But take a moment to think about what people lean on you for in your life. Identify those things that you make time for even when you're tired or busy. You may not have considered that that's what you could be doing with your whole life instead of it being this thing you reserve for the weekends.

God gives us a desire to have and work towards our purpose. I also believe that everyone desires to live a purpose-driven life. Rick Warren, the Pastor of Saddleback Christian Church, wrote a book titled Purpose Driven Life. It is a great resource for working through your purpose in about a month if you like that sort of thing. There is also a decent career planning book called What Color is My Parachute that has content designed to assist people as they try to figure out their professional purpose. I am not going to go into the level of detail of either of those books. The intention of bringing up your unique purpose here isn't to walk you through a detailed explanation of how to identify your "it." Instead, this is an attempt to convince you that everyone has a purpose, including you. Many people have more than one purpose throughout their lives. I hope to encourage you to set about finding out what your purpose is sometime before you die so that the world can be better because of it. More importantly, I have learned that knowing you are holy

---

[12] I do feel like I could have had a more enjoyable college experience studying elementary education or some equivalent. Just saying.

and have a purpose is critical in overcoming the unthinkable.

> Having gifts that differ according to the grace given to us, let us use them.

- ROMANS 12:6

Using our gifts and our unique talents is being holy. It does not matter what that gift is. Not everyone will have every gift and sometimes a person will have only one. The main point is that living in your purpose is being holy. It took me a long time to understand this. Although no one ever told me explicitly what they thought holy was, they certainly taught me what they believed holy should be. And that teaching involved a narrow definition that looked like a quiet, introverted, chaste, humorless prude without sex appeal. I was the opposite of all that and often felt less than holy. Which is unfortunate because I was showing up exactly how God made me to be. Because of years of feeling less than holy, I have an intention to help others tap into their unique holiness. I insist on helping others to see that unthinkable situations are not these things that you "will never get over" but they are the things that help you get over. But first I had to experience and see that for myself.

Today I own that I have a pure and authentic spirit. I have the gift of making people laugh and motivating people to be better through my words. It's my holy disposition and we all have it in some way. We simply have to embrace the wholly and holey parts of who we are as well.

WHOLLY

What does it mean to embrace ourselves wholly? We are each a sum of everything that has ever happened to us. Every single thing. If you change one thing, you might change it all. People often want to keep the wonderful parts of their pasts and wish to change the difficult or trying times. You can't do that. It's tempting to think that I would be richer, better off, less stressed or worried if I could just get rid of a bad decision here or there. That is an unproven and quite dangerous thought. While I think it is obvious why it is unproven, we also can't currently go back in history and take a different path. This "what if" thinking when looking in the past is dangerous because when we do it we are longing for a reality that just can't be.

For me, there are several things that I revisit when I'm not working from my elevated self. One that comes up for me often is what would my life be like if my daddy hadn't died when I was 10. I like to think that I was my father's favorite child[13]. We spent a lot of time together. He took me with him to the ballpark, he drove me to school, he allowed me to play with his treasured guitars, sometimes he even took me to work with him. I hear he was a volatile man at times but I never experienced him in that way. In my interactions with my father, he never so much as raised his voice with me. One particular memory stands out between us that I treasure deeply.

My dad was a truck driver and had a CB radio which was used for short-distance, person-to-person, two-way voice communication between people. It was like a walkie talkie but more sophisticated. I was enamored with the CB radio and I listened to my father talk with his friends on it many times when one day I decided I was going to use it. I was alone with the radio. I cleared my throat, pushed the side button, and said "Breaker, breaker one nine, this is Big Lou's baby girl."

---

[13] These are the kinds of things that good parents will not confirm.

"Breaker,
breaker,
1 - 9...
this is
Big Lou's
baby girl."

- ME

Then I let go of the button and waited for the responses. My dad overheard me from another room on a different CB radio so he came in laughing hysterically and encouraged me to keep talking.

I have forgotten more things about my father than I remember. However, when he died on my 10th birthday, all I could recall thinking was, "What am I going to do now?" The three years that he had been in hospitals and recovery centers are pretty much all a blur for me. I can't remember much about 3rd, 4th or 5th grade. I have suppressed the probable trauma of it all. I can vividly recount 2nd grade and 6th grade but all the time between is fuzzy; I don't remember much of anything from church, school or home. The only thing that stands out during that blank period is that I was over the Saturday morning hair frying ordeal forever. In a crying rage during the ritualistic hair tug of war, my mama asked if I just wanted to cut it all off. I said yes and before it was popular or considered cute, I had a big chop and was thrilled. My mother, who loved long, straight hair was probably relieved because during that time, she went to the hospital every day. She did not miss one day. Some of that time my dad was comatose and my mother was the only one convinced he was actually alive in that still body[14]. Her faithful love for my father came with a consequence. My little sister, who was a baby at the time, and I were left to the care of our other five siblings. Whatever happened, good or bad, I don't remember. What I do know is that sometimes I wonder how different things would be if I was afforded the opportunity to be raised by my daddy and my mama.

Here's the problem with that thinking though, if my dad had lived there are several other things that would not be true. You see, my dad's death was the result of medical malpractice. While his initial injuries were the result of him drinking while driving and crashing his car, he regained consciousness from his coma, regained more than half of his physical functions, and was

---

[14] My dad was in a coma for months and she refused to pull the plug because she said he responded to her. No one else saw these responses.

34

preparing to come home. We were literally planning our welcome home party when a basic trip to the dentist resulted in death. He was given too much anesthesia for a tooth extraction and died.

That day is clear because Mr. Joe, a neighbor, had organized an entire block party for my 10th birthday. This party was special because I had never had a birthday party before. Again, I was the 6th child of seven. When my dad had his accident, I was seven and my little sister was barely 6 months old. My nearest sibling was 11 years old. The one next to him was 14 years old and in trouble a lot. My middle sister already had two babies of her own. My oldest brother was married, had a toddler, and had left for the Army. And my oldest sister, and primary caretaker, had gotten married and left for Texas. Of course, I had never had a birthday party. It wasn't a priority.

But my tenth birthday was a blast. Everyone on the entire block was out for my big day. When the party was wrapping up I was across the street from my house still talking to Mr. Joe when I saw my mother being helped out of the car by my Uncle Rabbit. My Uncle Rabbit came over on Saturdays a lot so that wasn't odd but there was one thing dreadfully wrong with this picture, my mother was 40 years old and in great health, she didn't need or even want anyone physically helping her out of a car. I knew immediately – my dad was dead.

It's a sad story. When I was revisiting the moment in order to write this book, I cried. It was a very painful time. Here's the thing though, the wrongful death lawsuit that followed immediately got us out of poverty. For the first time, my mother had enough money to take care of all the basic essentials. She also could be a stay home mom. If I remove the death from my story, I have to add poverty and all of its challenges back in. While I would never choose to lose my dad for money, the money was a result of losing my dad.

Another point is that my parents were married as teenagers in Coahoma County Mississippi. They had seven children together and if all went along as it had been, they would likely still be together, meaning I would not have met a new "dad." A few years after my dad died, my mama dated another man. And while most of my siblings were pretty lukewarm toward him, I loved him and he loved me. He was very similar to my father in that he was also a truck driver. His CB handle was Engine No. 9 and my mama called him Nine. I'm pretty sure he and my dad had been friends or at least knew each other. That aside, he believed that caring for a woman meant pampering a woman and I had never seen anything like it before. He was a gift giver and his gifts of choice were trips to the salon but not for getting your hair done. He sent me to the salon for manicures, pedicures, and facials – at twelve. While he was a cook just like my father, he didn't teach me how to make southern food, his specialty was preparing a perfectly seared steak and grilled asparagus. He had served in the military, educated and I'm sure he encouraged my mother to allow me to explore new and different options often. With him, I got to travel and was exposed to many things I had never experienced before. He was not better than my father. For example, I don't believe I ever saw him fix anything, he paid for those services. He also wasn't a singer and musician, but he ensured we got to go to concerts. His hands were soft, he drove sports cars, and he was simply different in beautiful ways. Nine taught me to drive a standard shift, he drove me to college, he showed me what it looked like to be cared for, and he embraced me as the daughter he never had. If I remove the death of my biological father, for all that I think I would gain, I have to also assume I would never have met Nine.

It is enticing to think about how things would be different without certain deaths, unfortunately without certain births, with or without marriages or divorces, without pandemics, with different mentors, or with more information, without that injustice, with that money someone stole from you, without bouts of disease and mayhem, etc. I implore you to be careful with that thinking. If you change a variable the whole equation changes. "What if" thinking when we are looking back at the past, comes with a tinge of rose-colored tint. It is not a benefit to go back in history and to rewrite it in your favor. Every experience you have had has created the beautiful life you are given today.

The life we have is the only one we have to live. So we have to view the totality of our experiences like the ingredients to our favorite recipe. If you leave out one ingredient, the dish tastes different and likely worse.

The definition of living wholly is to embrace your whole life to this point in its entirety and fully. This is hard work but I invite you to think about the benefits to you for all of the major events in your

whol·ly /'hōl(1)ē/

adverb

entirely; fully.

life. This exercise is easy for the wonderful things that happened to us. It is harder for the more difficult life experiences we've had. To be clear, I am not asking you to practice positive psychology. Meaning, I am not asking you to go back in history and reconstruct an aspect of your life and create positive thoughts about horrible situations. Instead, I want you to think about how each experience has created the wonderful person you are today. For example, it isn't great that I woke up one day with $13.74 in my bank account when I thought I had thousands the previous day. However, because of that awful experience I have been able to truly empathize with many people, especially women, who have worked hard and made the best of opportunities, only to have them destroyed. I have been able to really be there for them as a trusted guide as they find their way out. I have also been able to serve as an example for a few people who have coined the term "Operation 1374." For them, my pain serves as a reminder that a setback does not mean the game is over. It simply means that you have experienced the unthinkable, you will get out of it, and better days are yet to come.

I long for my daddy sometimes. Whenever a man has ever talked to me with a gentle tone, whenever I hear the bass guitar, whenever I need something fixed, whenever I laugh and someone reacts to the uniqueness of my laughter, I miss my daddy. What has the loss of my father done for me? It has taught me that you can grow to be an amazing person with or without a father. When the whole world conspires to disparage single mothers, I think of how my mother held it down after my dad died and I stand strongly with single parents. When my own perfect image of a family was shattered by divorce, I knew one thing for sure – while it might not have been ideal, my child would be well and he would flourish. There were many times when other people would indirectly take jabs at my situation, so I get it. It can be tough dealing with the unthinkable but the way people can sometimes respond to you in those gutter moments can make a bad situation even worse. But the fortitude I had built internally was much stronger than any subtle shade anyone could manage to throw towards me and my son. You will find that when some unthinkable situation comes your way, you can build an armour of fortitude, too.

We live with regrets and what ifs sometimes. I, too, have dozens of not-so-great experiences that *IF* I could get a redo, I would likely take it or so I think. But when I evaluate what I have learned, what I have gained, how my life is better, stronger, kinder and gentler, I ditch that thinking. I embrace and accept the life I have as the beautiful one I have been blessed to live. Painful and unthinkable experiences are rarely, if ever, welcomed. I haven't gotten to the place where I welcome the unthinkable. What has happened is that I have come to see that the high moments have not been the ones to give me depth and substance. But rather it has been the midnight fire call, the deportation struggle, the death, the pain, the hurt—the unthinkables that built the strength of my resolve. Hang on to this idea when you are in the middle of your own unthinkable situation.

For now, evaluate the formidable experiences in your life to this point. How have they helped you live your current purpose? How have those experiences shaped you? How have they created more depth of character? How have they allowed you to show up authentically for others? The answers to these questions will help you live a wholly life. It is a whole life lived by you – a "holey" person.

HOLEY

The holy part of being a holy, educated motherf*cker is being the master and leader of your own life. It is also fully embracing yourself, the good and the bad (holey), because both are necessary for your purpose. At a training workshop early in my career, I was formally introduced to personality instruments. Looking back it's obvious I was different, but at the time I didn't see it. I wasn't blue-collar enough to fit in with my family, and my personality was too colorful to fit in with the starched white-collar engineering environment. Not until I began participating in and studying personality assessments for myself did I realize just how different the beat was that I marched to and that for me it was less about wealth and more about basic wiring. Whenever I take an assessment that is not scientifically validated, it can be a bit confusing because I am a social butterfly who is great with science and math. I am also logical and reasonable. By association, unvalidated personality instruments that you might find on the internet usually return a result that suggests that I am also detail oriented and methodical. Nope, I am not. I can feign that I have those skills but only because I spent the largest part of my formative years with people who were determined to make me be detail oriented and methodical. People tend to think that those specific skills are necessary to be successful. In fact, after I had completed engineering school, was gainfully employed and leading other people, gotten a terminal degree, raised a decent human, and successfully started a business, a friend still questioned how it was possible that I could be successful without being a J on the Myers Briggs. In case you don't know, Js are the planful, early-starting, methodical, list makers and box checkers.

39

After that first workshop though, I could no longer deny that I am not a planful person. I'm not even close and the model they used was scientifically validated with millions of participants. Besides the science, I literally find little to no enjoyment in planning out every detail of my life. In fact, if I have to plan my free time, I get annoyed. The quote, "plan your work and work your plan" doesn't resonate with me as much as the quote "people plan and God laughs." In all honesty, my best ideas come to me at the last minute. Interestingly, when I have an idea I have to jump right in and strike when the iron is hot otherwise, I will stall. But when I am not operating at a higher level of consciousness, I envy people who are methodical and plan out their approaches. Those people with their little[15] checklists serve as a mirror of comparison for me. And you know how that adage goes, "Comparison is the enemy of all joy." Even though I know that, I also feel like things would go better if I didn't change things at the ninth hour.

But here's the thing, we need planful people and we need more casual and spontaneous people. We need all kinds of people. The world would have you believe that certain kinds of people are better than others. If you aren't careful you will buy-in to the idea that people who think for a living are better than those who work with their hands. You can easily fall into the belief that scientists are more important than artists. You can be lulled into thinking that people who are detail oriented are more skilled than people who are more conceptual and big picture thinkers.

Here's what you should know, no matter how amazing a person is, they have an Achilles heel. There are things we are all good at and things we struggle with – we have holes. Holes don't make us incomplete. All humans are solid, fully functioning bodies with "hollow places" or areas where we simply don't have will, skill, talent or ability to perform. That is the definition of holey.

[15] See what I did there?

40

hol·ey

/ˈhōl(l)ē/

adjective

full of holes; describes a solid
body that has hollow places

Your ability to embrace your holes without ignoring
them altogether is imperative. It will help you be a more
empathetic person; being more understanding when someone
has a gap in their personal approaches. It will help you better
understand why some people are passionate about certain
things and others are not. More importantly, it will inform
why YOU are passionate about some things and not others.

PASSION

Passion fuels the effort engine. It is what keeps you going
when others would get tired and quit. Passion provides you
with the needed resilience in the face of the unthinkable. I have
asked thousands of people what gets in the way of their ability
to be consistently effective. One answer that always makes the
list is "lack of time." Time is hardly of consequence when it's
something you are passionate about. Think for a moment about
the end to a very trying day. Now imagine your friend offered
you an opportunity of a lifetime. Would you pass on it because
you were tired? Most people would not. A poet once said that
wholeheartedness is the antidote to fatigue. Wholeheartedness
or passion ignites our stamina. Weariness and fatigue can be
combated by making sure you are spending most of your time

41

working in areas where you have genuine passion for the work.

Regardless of where your passion lies, understand that your passion will come with "holes." It is rare to find an excellent writer who is also an amazing orator. A person who misses no detail when reviewing a legal document is not usually the most innovative strategist. A risk taker is not likely to enjoy the routine associated with a task-driven job that is the same day-in and day-out. Your job is to align your passion with work and volunteer interests where your "holes" are not requirements for the role or find a partner whose holes are different from your holes who can complement you and your skill set.

Take a moment to identify your strengths and your holes. Ask yourself which strength is automatically associated with a hole. As an example, I am a questioning, critical thinker by nature which lends itself to me having an issue with creating harmony and agreeability. Clearly, I can't question people all the time and expect them to label me as agreeable. On the other hand, agreeable people are incredibly likable but often struggle to get what they need by over-using collaboration. List your top three strengths and then list the opposite of those strengths (holes). How can you find ways to add value in spaces where those holes simply aren't a requirement?

What does this have to do with overcoming the unthinkable? In my professional life, I often encounter people who have found me because they have been fired. Being terminated from a job, especially when it wasn't performance based, can be disorienting. It is an unthinkable situation because we are trained to believe that people who get fired have performance issues; not their work but them. When people find me in their brokenness, sometimes a person they love has left them. Heartbreak is another hard situation to deal with because when we fall in love we don't imagine a life whereby we hate our love interest or they hate us. Unfortunately, this is a common outcome of breakups. Both instances of termination, in work and in love, are unthinkable situations. However, if you stick with me, you will find that there are jobs whereby your new colleagues love the very thing you were terminated for in your previous role. In romance, you will find a love that suits your holey personality quirks better than a tailored suit. Believe this with everything you have. It is part of the process of overcoming. Trust me on this and know that you won't even have to close a bunch of gaps in your portfolio of experiences. Someone, somewhere, will like your "holes."

HOLEY EXPERIENCES

Holes show up in different ways other than merely as personality gaps. Holes show up as gaps in experiences, too. The difference is that you can't control most aspects of your personality. You can get a coach, go to therapy, etc. and get to a point where your personality holes aren't as detrimental to you but good luck with changing them. Now, that's a rule and before you start listing the handful of people you know throughout history who have changed their personality, understand that exceptions always underscore the rule. As a rule, it doesn't happen. However, holes in experiences can be remedied if you want.

As a personal example, I have never lived outside the United States. I also don't have a lot of experiences living in many cities in the United States. These two points mean that unless I move, there is no way for me to understand the experience of a child raised in the military who moved with their family every year. It also means that I cannot be a representative of an immigrant's experience. How could I? My lived experiences are only as a United States citizen and that experience is limited to less than a handful of cities. Just as everyone has holes in their personality, everyone has holes in their lived experiences as well.

Holes in your lived experiences are also nothing to cause you to pause unless you need that specific experience to be successful in some way. When I think about the small ways other people will try to use holes in your experiences to prove or disprove validation, I think about how once at work someone was singing the words to Boot Scootin' Boogie and I sang along.

43

My co-worker went on and on expressing his shock and awe. He even went so far as to engage other people in the conversation. Want to know why I know the words to Boot Scootin' Boogie? Well, I was a model in high school and that song was chosen as one of the offerings for the Ralph Lauren line. I had to listen to it over and over and over again during the back-to-school marketing period as I sashayed down a runway. My knowing that song is no indication of my experience with or love for Brooks & Dunn. In fact, I couldn't tell you any of their other songs. For me these kinds of situations are of no consequence because for everything I haven't experienced, there's an entirely different group of things I have. You see, I could have named the top 100 greatest Gospel hits, sang them all word for word, and he would have had no knowledge of any of them. Does that mean he has holes in his experience that are insurmountable? Not at all unless he needs to know that information. Everyone has holes in their lived experiences. There are two reasons for you to remember this. One is so that you don't feel the need to hold yourself to this ridiculous standard of having experienced everything. That will hinder you and be a detriment to the mindset you need when faced with the unthinkable. And two, remember so that you never look at another person and say something like, "Whaaaaaaat? You've never been to Fiji? That's going to be a problem." Conventional wisdom says that you can't possibly be something you have never seen or experienced before. The holy, educated motherf*cker says that is a limiting belief that ignores the entire concept of innovation and the power of the human mind to craft ideas seemingly from nothing. There is nothing like an unthinkable situation to remind us that "necessity is the mother of invention."

Remember holy you, wholly you, and holey you all represent you. Each aspect of you is more than alright, each should be celebrated. There are things you will not know because you haven't had certain experiences. That doesn't mean that you are less than anyone else. People learn many things through experiences. It's called experiential learning. The more you experience the more you realize there is to experience. There is no end to experiential learning opportunities. They might make you more

"Heel toe do si do

Come on baby let's go
boot scootin'

Oh cadillac blackjack
baby meet me out back

We're gonna boogie

Oh, get down,
turn around,
go to town

Boot scootin' boogie"

- BROOKS & DUNN

interesting to some people. They may make you less interesting to others. Therefore, when you embark on new experiences because of an attempt to close a hole in your life, be sure you are doing so because you value the experience. Beware of the very human temptation to engage in these activities because you are trying to be impressive to someone else. It begins this cycle of inauthenticity that is hard to overcome. In the communities where I identify, we call it fake and no one trusts a fake. Besides, living a fake life is living a lie. That is not very holy of you.

chapter three

Educated

ed·u·cat·ed

/'ejə͵kādəd/

adjective

person who has gone through the process
of receiving or giving systematic instruction,
especially at a school or university

Prior to second grade, I missed school regularly and had trouble
reading. However, my second grade teacher, Mr. Thomas, identified
that I actually learned well in traditional settings and could perform
science and math problems with little issue. As such, Mr. Thomas
worked with me to improve my reading and invited me to be
responsible for my own attendance in school so that he could use
the time to teach me algebraic concepts. I had a consistent ride
to school but pick-up time after school was demanding for my
parents who both worked and who had five other children at the
time, one on the way, and often depended on one car. Based on Mr.
Thomas's nudging, I asked my parents if I could catch the city bus
home from school. My dad asked me to tell him the route, I was
able to do so, and he said yes. Frequently for the first part of the
school year before my dad's accident, I navigated a 30-minute walk
and bus ride from my elementary school to my house at age seven.

From as early as I could remember, I hated missing school. I
didn't like it when I was behind. And I did everything I could in
order to get all A's. Looking back, I think it was because my mother
didn't get to attend school. She was so smart but was raised by her
maternal grandmother who believed that the cotton harvest was
more important than going to school. My mother didn't like being

48

behind either and starting school every year after the harvest was over was just enough for her to decide that she would rather not deal with the embarrassment of trying to catch up academically. I mean can you imagine a knapsack around your waist and trekking up and down dirt rows picking cotton when you're supposed to be in kindergarten, first, or second grade? I can't but in third grade my mama chose the cotton field every day to avoid the shame of school. My mama told these stories over and over again when I was little. I was embarrassed for her and we had the aversion to embarrassment in common. The only difference was that I never missed months of school at a time, I just missed a day here or there so I could catch up. My absences also were not because my mama didn't value education. It wasn't like I was picking cotton instead of going to school. Things simply come up when you are poor that get in the way of basic things like getting the kids to and from school consistently. I loved school because the privilege wasn't afforded to my mama but I loved school for other reasons, too. Other people responded to academic excellence in ways that fueled my spirit. Once the church was paying students for getting A's. No one had considered that I didn't really get Bs and the church quickly changed that practice when they had to give me $100. That was a point of personal pride. At one point, I expressed to people that I wanted to be valedictorian. The responses I received were like jet fuel to my desire engine but I wasn't enrolled in enough AP courses and it just wasn't in the cards for me. As high school was ending, I adjusted my goal to simply being in the top 10% of my class. That didn't happen either. I was in the top 15% of my class, which for my small high school probably wasn't that impressive but it was enough for a full engineering scholarship. It was also enough for most people to still be impressed. It is tempting to think that I could have done much better if someone would have been pushing me but we've already gone over what is wrong with that line of thinking.

I loved learning. I specifically enjoyed asking questions. Sometimes it would get me in trouble, even in church. When I was a pre-teen I was essentially kicked out of junior Sunday School for asking too many questions. Consequently, I was enrolled in the

49

young adult class. Brother Sam Harper was the instructor. Everyone in class called him Uncle Sam which often made me giggle inside[16]. I loved the young adult class. When I would ask questions, Uncle Sam had an answer or knew where to tell me to look. If he didn't do either of those, he would explain the historical context of an idea. He was known for saying regularly, "Do not agree with me because I am your teacher." For once, I had an intellectual as a Sunday school teacher and I could not get enough. The students in the class were older and smarter than me, too and often they would ask questions about life that were beyond my immediate interest but not beyond my understanding. One day someone told Uncle Sam that they did not need a formal education beyond high school. He was physically unmoved. In general, he didn't move fast anyway. Uncle Sam had a gravitas about him that was comforting and grounding. In his typical fashion, he asked a question,

"What does a formal education gain you?"

He asked it like a riddle but with a suggestive tone that insinuated the answer was "nothing." I didn't know the answer so I just listened as other students said things like more money, better jobs, greater opportunities, etc. Then Uncle Sam said, "You don't have to get any formal education after high school." I did not expect that from him so I was attentive but shocked. Then he followed up with, "A formal education allows you to be mobile." He went on to explain that if you were a hairdresser in one town with dozens of clients and then you wanted to move to another town, a cosmetology license would give you the credentials to start over in your new town. He said that without the license people wouldn't trust you to style their hair. The formal education makes people give you their trust if they don't know you or your work. The class kept talking about it because that one person just didn't want anything to do with more schooling. I mentally checked out. I was stuck on that notion that higher education gives you additional mobility

---

[16] Tall, Black, heavy, and with a purposefully unkempt Afro, Sam looked nothing like the caricature of Uncle Sam.

and trust. At the time I hadn't been to many places. I had been to school. I had been to church including a few churches in my region. I had been to a few stores. And I had visited my grandma via car so it would seem that I had at least seen all the cities along the 8-hour route but I had not. My biological parents liked to drive at night and from a young age, my body has desired sleep at around 9:00 PM. I always slept through the whole trip missing all the gas station stops. Consequently, I had not seen much before Nine started allowing me to drive across the country with him. So I was excited about having a way to change my mobility through education.

When you are faced with overcoming the unthinkable, it is helpful if you have some credentials that render you mobile and trustworthy. There's a certain confidence that comes with knowing that no matter what happens you have a skill that can take you lots of places and that people trust you to provide that skill for them. The world has changed drastically since Uncle Sam made that statement to a class full of hopeful young people. There are now many ways outside of formal education to demonstrate your talent. What has not changed is that in many instances the access point is still your curriculum vitae. In some cases, you just can't get around the credentialing. Of course there are exceptions and some of those exceptions are astounding to me. As an engineer, your credentials lead. I was quite shocked when I shifted over to the social sciences and started working in the area of diversity. There I learned that people will hire someone to conduct diversity, and even race work, without any verification that validates their cultural proficiency[17]. That simply doesn't happen in technical fields and can be maddening at times because lives are at stake in both cases.

Regardless, education is never enough. Education must be accompanied by access and opportunity and I was blessed with my fair share. After all, I had Mr. Thomas as a teacher who was a culturally responsive educator far before the term was

---

[17] Can you imagine a person who is culturally destructive teaching your inclusion class? I couldn't either before I started doing this work.

51

popular. I value formal education, however, it can be tricky. I think people should be allowed to study things that will benefit them that also align with their personality. When I was offered an engineering scholarship, it was inevitable that I would accept it even though my personality vehemently disagreed.

From the time I was spending with Mr. Thomas, math and science were easier for me to understand than they were for other students. Because I was a girl, Black, and also a first generation college student, I don't recall being encouraged to do much else. The only exception is the one time a counselor suggested social work as my potential field of study. That was laughable. If you think I am crass now, you should have seen what my mouth was like in high school. I don't have the temperament to be a social worker today and I certainly didn't have the empathy and compassion to do so back then. That counselor was an exception and I don't know what was wrong with her[18]. Whatever it was, she certainly was not a good talent matcher. In contrast, most people pushed me towards the sciences and encouraged me to be an engineer. Interestingly, I literally had no idea what an engineer did at the time and that did not change until I got my first assignment as a chemical engineering intern. That didn't matter because I had a plethora of opportunities in high school. I understand that in order to catapult from poverty, a person has to experience several years with no major negative or unthinkable events[19]. That was me. From 12 - 17 years old not one thing went horribly wrong that had a negative impact on my trajectory. That is nothing more than the universe conspiring in my favor, blessings, and opportunity.

In high school, I had access to many teachers who believed in me. My AP literature professor, Ms. Elaine Scholzman, inadvertently christened me. She was totally perplexed at how someone coming from my given environment and circumstances, still had any enthusiasm for learning. Even though my middle

---

[18] Actually, I do. Poor students are always shifted towards social work.

[19] Peter Temin economist from MIT

52

and high school had selective admission, and many of the students had free and reduced lunch, I'm not sure they all had my tumultuous living arrangements. Still, I liked to debate. I was a ravenous reader with unique tastes. Albert Camus was one of my favorites. I was also into Nietzsche and Naughty by Nature, Carter G. Woodson's The Mis-Education of the Negro later informed my love for The Mis-Education of Lauryn Hill. Yet, it would be nothing for me to prepare a commencement address after a 5-day suspension for fighting. I had an outrageous way of interpreting and communicating that was as entertaining as it was thorough. She called me a "lively paradox" – intellectually stimulating, and a seemingly absurd or self-contradiction. Before that label, being different had never been articulated in a way that sounded in any way appealing to me. My difference often translated in my mind as a confliction. Ms. Scholzman opened my eyes and her description served as an opportunity for me to accept myself. This was an acceptance I needed when I left Kansas City to go attend undergrad at North Carolina Agricultural and Technical State University (Ayantee) in Greensboro, North Carolina.

My best friend, Brandy, and I chose Ayantee by drawing names out of a hat. It's a terrible way to pick a college but that's exactly what we did. We knew we wanted to attend a historically Black college or university. We also knew that we wanted to be far away from Kansas City. Third, she was pretty certain that she wanted to be a chemical engineer. Me? Well, I didn't know the difference between the engineering fields and thought that maybe I wanted to be a chemist or a physicist[20]. Those three criteria left us with Prairie View A&M State University in Texas, Florida A&M State University, and Ayantee. We wrote the names on little strips of paper, placed them in a container, and pulled a name out. The first selection was Florida A&M.

[20] I didn't know what they did either but stating "physicist" was met with ooohh and ahhhh.

53

Me : *Ok. Ok. Wait! How were we choosing?*

Brandy : *We are going with two out of three.*

Me : *Ok so not FAMU yet?*

Brandy : *No. Two out of three.*

Me : **Shakes the container and leans it towards her to pull twice more**

Brandy : *So it's FAMU? *with a lot of trepidation in her voice**

Me : *Let's do it again.*

Brandy : *Ok!*

Me : *Put FAMU back in. *Shakes the container and leans it towards her again**

She pulled Ayantee on the first two tries and we were excited we were headed to Greensboro. The next few days were filled with a flurry of phone calls and making arrangements. It was the spring of senior year and both of us had other plans that weren't going to work out so we were just happy to be together. Her father had just passed away and at 17, I was able to be there for her because I had been grieving my dad for seven years by then and could relate.

Even though I was a late add, North Carolina A & T State University wanted me. Specifically the engineering school had keen interest. I started out in the Chemistry School and changed swiftly because the dean of the chemical engineering program was more tenacious. I recall when we first arrived on campus. It was much bigger than I had imagined. I was thinking about how the civil right activist Rev. Jesse Jackson had walked these specific streets. I also thought about the courage of the Greensboro Four and I felt a sense of pride that I, too, would be a graduate from this illustrious institution. What stood out to me more than anything else was

54

how friendly people were. Every person I saw looked me in my face, smiled, and said hello. Everywhere I looked there was Black skin; thousands of Black people all around me and everybody was helpful, kind and generous. The campus was also beautifully plush and green. It had the warmth of Coahoma County, Mississippi but with an intellectual snobbery that enveloped me. I felt I was at home.

Nine dropped off my stuff and returned to Kansas City leaving my mom and Brandy's mom there to take care of the fine tuning. Our dorm was Vanstory Hall and Brandy and I were together on the first floor in the same room. Brandy's brother had worked miracles on the phone to not only get us in the same dorm but in the same room. Our mamas successfully transformed our room from a sterile box to a beautiful little sanctuary. The process took all day and they looked tired so Brandy and I took them to the hotel to rest. The next morning when we went back to pick them up for breakfast, they were already in Kansas City. They left without even saying goodbye. Once I dropped my own child off at college, I understood why she left me in that way - she could not take the pain. I wanted to cry but I felt I had to keep it together in front of my friend. In that moment I redirected my energy towards what was in front of me. This was not a sad occasion. We had done it. We decided to go to Ayantee by ourselves, thousands of miles from home, and now this was our reality.

Ayantee was it's own little city—Black city. I had never seen anything like it. Everything I ever wanted was there for me. From the food I loved to the products I needed for my hair, everything I needed was within reach. I didn't have to go to a special part of town. I didn't need to find that one particular restaurant. There was no need to look around in the drugstore for makeup or pantyhose in my skin tone. It was all there. On that campus I met the children of farmers with massive tobacco acreage, doctors, entertainers, professors, astronauts, politicians, and mega pastors. I met people who were first generation college students like me. I met people who were second generation college students like Brandy but I also met many people whose great grandparents were students at

Ayantee and my mind was opened. All the older Black people I had met to that point had some sort of limited educational experience. Not here. Here students came from long lineages of educational excellence. All of a sudden, I was thrust into an environment where I had my share of issues but my skin color wasn't one of them. If I had a terrible instructor, they were just terrible. I could bet everything I had at the time that if there was an issue with my professors, it most certainly wasn't because they were bigots. For one of the first times in my life I was smart and that wasn't a delineator. Academic excellence and brilliance was all around me by the thousands. Another thing that was prevalent was the range of faith traditions— various denominations of Christians including Catholics, Muslims, Black Hebrews, agnostics and atheists. It was the first time I had to test my religious openness. I passed except for one time.

Brandy and I noticed that there was a church right across the street from campus—The United House of Prayer. One of our first Sundays in Greensboro we went to visit. By all accounts it seemed like a normal church then we noticed that this Daddy Grace character they kept referencing wasn't actually there nor was he coming. Later we learned that these devout followers believed that the long deceased Sweet Daddy Grace was the coming of the Messiah and were convinced that he possessed the power of God to heal the sick and raise the dead[21]. We sat in the pews for what felt like three hours listening to the recounting of this belief in various ways. I still loved church but in college realized that church, no matter the faith tradition, doesn't have to take all day. Besides, I need a stretch break at around the 90-minute mark. We snuck out and never went back.

I learned more things at Ayantee than I could ever formally capture. This random decision that wasn't planned was a formidable force in my life then and still is today. In fact, whenever the

[21] It was theologically similar to what Christians believe about Jesus but something about the empty chair in the pulpit didn't land with my spirit. It was an illogical resistance.

56

weight of institutional racism and its associated stress gets to me, I venture back to Homecoming. Throwing myself in the middle of nothing but Black bodies and engulfing myself in the cocoon of the Black college alumni experience. A mere three days is enough to give me the inoculation I need from the racist world for an entire year until I need my booster. Food, music, dance, fashion, all there seemingly just to reinvigorate my mind, body, and soul. The education I received was rigorous and there was no level of surprise or awe when I lived up to the expectation. I may have been able to gain the academics elsewhere, but I believe there is nowhere else in the states for a Black college student to get an amazing education and keep her soul intact except for at an HBCU.

I don't ever mention my educational pursuits in order to contribute to the narrative of American exceptionalism. While I do believe in the value of self-reliance, the inflated importance given to individualism and rugged independence is a tall tale that's doing more harm than good at this point. I share Mr. Thomas's and Ms. Scholzman's accounts because they happened in grammar and high school. That means I knew, or at least had an idea, since way back when that I was on a different path. It took me some time to fully accept it. But back then I wasn't willing to be different yet. I wasn't ready to let my proverbial "freak flag" fly because I might be saluting it on my own. So, despite all the signs to the contrary, I spent many more years in lockstep with the expected—engineering.

I find engineering to be interesting. That fact should have been the end of my journey but it wasn't. I studied engineering for four years. Interned as an engineer, worked as a project engineer, production engineer, research engineer, wastewater engineer, printing engineer, and process improvement engineer. It's almost like I couldn't get it. As an example, there is one photo of me with my engineering peers dressed for a business dinner. There I am, right in the middle of all of them in an off-white pantsuit. Them? All dressed in navy and black. That one picture demonstrates the problem—I am not an engineer. Well, once an engineer always an engineer but my personality never agreed. Based on outcomes,

I was a good engineer, though. It's just that my methods were unconventional based on the ways engineers typically approach things. To other engineers, I wasn't doing engineering right. To them, engineers are always the experts in their fields. On the other hand, I never wanted to be an expert in any engineering process. I simply wanted to know enough about the processes I supported to be able to know who I needed to partner with who was already an expert. My engineering approach was to bring cross-sections of people together to get to a better solution faster. I was just different in many ways you could not physically observe but I was also different in ways you could see. I was one of three women on the leadership team in that production plant and the other two were both lesbian. I was also one of only two Black people on the leadership team wearing my hair in natural dreadlocks well before the Crown Act had been passed. Not to be overlooked, I was also younger than most people there had been working and my colleagues nearest to me in age were at least 15 years my senior. In some ways, I imagine that my cultural background and familial upbringing strongly influenced my thinking. Regardless, I just couldn't understand the purpose of having dozens of experts on a single process. This thinking got me in trouble often enough but there's a specific instance that stands out.

Jim Shockey wasn't an engineer. In fact, he didn't have a degree at all. He was rough around the edges, smoked like a chimney, and cursed like a sailor. However, Shockey was a printing expert. There were a few printing experts that did not work directly on the production floor. Two of them were engineers—Homer and Paul. Homer, a fan of Bluegrass, was conversant in flexography printing and Paul, a military vet, was familiar with gravure printing which was an older but higher quality printing process. With all that expertise, I didn't see the need in me wasting 20 years of my life becoming a printing expert as well. So one time I needed expert printing advice in a meeting and I invited Shockey to attend the meeting with me. Solves the issue, right? Shockey knew both flexography and gravure printing in a practical sense more than anyone in that production facility. Consequently, I

58

didn't even think about it and I certainly didn't ask if it was ok. Shockey was educated. He wasn't an engineer but he was educated in printing. There was only one problem with my decision to invite him to the meeting. That's just not how things were done.

I maintain it was one of the smartest things I ever did. You have to pull diverse thoughts together if you want to be smarter. A group of engineers alone is a pretty monolithic group. You can gain incredible insight from having a Shockey in the room and part of the entire conversation rather than getting his perspective and buy-in second hand. As a result of this type of thinking, I was consistently seen as a renegade and irresponsible but one year Paul and I were specifically chosen to assist with major cost savings and I could have used Shockey.

ed·u·ma·cat·ed

/'e jooˏmah kādəd/

adjective

Black Urban Vernacular; having an informal PhD or terminal degree in common sense

At that time, the gravure printing was done in one building where we would print 40-ft rolls of stock, stack the rolls up, and store them until they needed to be converted in an entirely different building across the street. I wasn't a printing expert but I knew that this process was wasteful from watching my mama and my maternal grandma cook. Both of them regularly cooked for dozens of people but my mother cooked on a production line. She had been a cafeteria worker in a sizable high school and was responsible for the food ministry at our church. In both cases, I learned a lot about cost, efficiency, high quality, and waste reduction from observing a food service production line. From those experiences I learned that you would never cook one part of your meal, store it, and then assemble it with another part of your meal later and in a different building if you were feeding a large group of people. Besides being woefully inefficient, now you have added unnecessary levels of complexity to an otherwise straightforward process. How would you inventory it? How would you keep track of use-by dates? Maybe you could do this on a small scale but never in large quantities if you are cooking every day. In our plant we were basically cooking in large quantities every day and finishing the preparation in another building across the street. There were elaborate transportation and storage systems in place. I felt it was ridiculous. Therefore, I took my edumacation from the kitchen and had a conversation with Paul to solve our cost savings issue. This is a snippet of the conversation:

Me : *Paul, we should move the gravure presses.*

Paul : **Blank stare**

Me : *Hear me out, Paul. We should turn them all 90 degrees, running them the length of the plant moving the converting equipment from across the street to the end of each press.*

Paul : **Laughing* Gravure presses run at 1,000 ft/ min and the converting equipment is much slower.*

Me : *I know but I've run the numbers and for what we would save in waste at the beginning and end of the printed rolls, lost or damaged inventory, transportation, space, insurance cost, and labor makes up for the dollars we lose by slowing down the printing to match the converting speed.*

Paul : *Let me see your numbers, grasshopper.*

Me : *Shows him an ROI of over 90% and conservative savings of $10 million*

Paul : *You just don't move gravure presses.*

Me : *Have you ever moved them?*

Paul : *Yes. *Laughing some more* Put your presentation together.*

The parent company's founder believed in simplicity. He said that if you couldn't explain your idea on a 3 x 5 note card, that meant you did not understand it well enough. Although the founder passed away in 1982, I had heard he felt this way from many people who still remained at the company decades later. In employee orientation, we all learned about this thinking because it explained why the company still had high quality, blank 3 x 5 cards always available for notes and possible innovative ideas[22]. At times, I think I took this more simplistic approach too literally.

In the spirit of Simon Sinek well before I knew who he was, I decided to start with why, share the idea simply, and speak from and to the heart. When I gave that presentation to the plant engineering management from both buildings, I never even got to the "head" or numbers part of my presentation. I was basically laughed out of the room. It was 10 years before they would do exactly what I recommended. Ten years later, not only did they turn the gravure presses, they moved them across the street to the other building and Paul was the lead engineer[23]! I was long gone and I still think about the years of wasted money and time. What gets at me the most wasn't that they didn't do the project when I suggested. What was more of an issue for me is that it was my personality that was getting in the way. What inspires me must motivate me so I tried to treat my audience the way I wanted to be treated instead of

---

[22] Why did I miss those note cards more than anything else when I got a new job?

[23] I guess although he didn't offer much support during my failed presentation, he was paying attention.

treating them how they wanted to be treated. I didn't pivot and think about what would be inspiring to them—spreadsheets and diagrams. Because I was trying to inspire them around the idea before getting to the nitty gritty details, I could not convince them. As such, no huge bonus for me or Shockey who completely knew how to implement my ridiculous idea when I first thought of it ten years prior but I couldn't bring him to my meetings anymore.

The edumacation that both Shockey and I had from various places was proven to be beneficial even if it were a decade later. That delayed response wasn't an indication of true value but of perceived value. The challenge for the edumacated is concerning ourselves with ensuring that perception matches reality. Good sense and sound judgment on practical matters is as valuable as theoretical or academic prowess. edumacation is in plain terms like having a PhD in common sense. People like me will ditch the academics when it flies in the face of good, old common sense. I am not saying engineers don't have common sense. What I am saying is that sometimes for everything they tend to have in expertise, sometimes they can't just take the learnings they got from watching their mamas cook. A crazy idea that doesn't follow the process or convention is dismissed. Furthermore, the simplest solutions are often overlooked for more complicated mechanical options that demonstrate engineering capabilities rather than simply solve a problem. As an example, sometimes a dry erase board will do the trick and a highly computerized display is visually impressive but cumbersome and inefficient. However for all the pain of engineering, there were far more benefits than there were liabilities associated with choosing that degree focus. Many of those benefits come in the form of subtle privileges I experience as soon as someone learns that I am an engineer. People are still impressed today and I get interesting opportunities because of it.

When you are faced with the unthinkable, use whatever you have at your disposal to help you find your way out. Whether it be an educational experience that you don't value as much anymore or rather it is an informal learning experience you've had, lean on the

62

strength of all of it. You will need it when your opportunity arises.

OPPORTUNITIES

Just moseying through a career fair, I ran into some recruiters from my hometown who were ecstatic to give me an engineering job fresh out of college with a meager 3.0 GPA. I said I didn't want to work in a plant, and they ditched all their rules to give me my first experience at corporate. They also gave me the salary I requested. When I had the 1374 fiasco, it was the engineering role that was instrumental in helping me avoid termination when my business credit card had been used. I was in a reputable role. When I went to talk with my engineering manager about the unauthorized charge on my corporate card, she didn't flinch. She told me that I could pay it myself and basically suggested that there was no harm, so no foul. Do you really believe I would get that kind of grace as a cafeteria worker? I can't know for sure, but I do know that I have since learned of a decent number of people who have gotten fired for similar infractions. That was an opportunity. She gave me an opportunity to right a wrong. Everyone, especially those in underrepresented groups, can't say that they get these kinds of breaks.

When I got my first shot at executive leadership, everyone on the search committee wasn't quite convinced. The main holdout completely changed his tune once he realized I had an undergraduate degree in chemical engineering. He went from a hard and emphatic "No" to "She must be pretty brilliant if she was able to finish such a tough curriculum." He closed his interview folder and started asking personal questions. Yes, I was qualified for the role before his revelation. But I don't make that statement because I am any better than anyone else necessarily. However, his change of heart was more because of implicit biases and associations. At times people have given me opportunities because the word engineering causes people to think I am like Paul and Homer in some very specific, engineering ways that I am not.

Once I decided that I didn't want to work in engineering

anymore and set out to find a new career that aligned to my personality better, I received opportunities right away. People assume that if you can complete an engineering degree that you must at least be smart enough to learn other jobs. As such,when I identified a position in the learning and development field, by the luck of professional relationships, I got the job with very little[24] formal experience in the role. I am grateful for the people who have given me opportunities. I just hate it when there is this insinuation that education alone accounts for success. Education must meet opportunity.

However, when you get an opportunity, it is important that you don't waste it. I did not waste my opportunities. Even though I had minimal experience in HR and none in learning and development, I was a natural. I loved to teach and coach. Conducting leadership training came naturally for me and it is still one of my favorite things to do. As such, it could have been tempting to just rest on natural talent and not hone the craft. You have to resist that urge.

I embarked on a journey to become more credible by obtaining my masters in adult education. I took all the classes I could to learn about what it takes to make for a decent learning environment for the participants in my classes. I became a certified coach, I read every book on leadership development that was placed in front of me, and I practiced on the job every chance I got. Today I have earned an educational doctorate in leadership and management. So here's what I know about engineering; it was not that I didn't value expertise, I didn't value expertise in printing. However, no one had to give me an opportunity to transition careers and try out learning and development. When people act like individualism and education alone accounts for their success, I am skeptical. That skepticism comes because I know that everyone who is successful has had some luck, access or been given an opportunity that catapulted their journey. No woman or man is an island and accomplished great feats by pulling her/

---

[24] Little = no as in none, zilch, or nada.

himself up by the bootstraps. If they did, someone at least gave him some boots. When someone offers you an opportunity, say 'yes." In the gutter you have to be especially attuned to your confidence level because when the unthinkable happens your self-esteem will likely take a hit. Will yourself into the belief that if you are given an opportunity that means you can do it if you want to. Now if you don't want to, that's an easy no.

During the unthinkable there will also be opportunities for you to be generous to other people, as well. Contrary to popular belief, the gutter is not the real gutter. I expect educated people to own this and pay back what has been graciously given to them. There is always someone else in a lower place, some even in an actual gutter. Giving to them will help your spirit. During your unthinkable crisis moments, you will find opportunities for you to share and offer access to other people. Do it! During this time it might seem like you need to hunker down and focus on self. Instead, I invite you to open up and see the value in community; a community that includes a few Khalilahs and Shockeys. You will be smarter because of it and the generosity flowing from your heart will fuel you, too.

SMARTS

I mention my educational pursuits not to encourage you to obtain a terminal degree and certainly not to get you to be impressed with mine. But rather, I write about education because no matter what your purpose is or what you are passionate about, you need to be intelligent, knowledgeable, or smart when an opportunity arises. There are nine ways to be intelligent or smart; this list can be seen on the next page.

Whichever type of intelligence comes naturally for you, it is important to work even harder at being formally informed in those areas. We can balk about the merits and effectiveness of the educational system but when faced with the unthinkable, try getting up and out of it without some experience and savviness in the basic tenets of how the system of education works and you will

65

Intelligence	Definition
PEOPLE	sensing people's feelings and emotions
LIFE	tackling the questions of why we live and why we die
PERSONAL	understanding yourself, what you feel, and what you want
BODY	coordinating your body with your mind
LINGUISTIC	finding the right words to express what you mean
REASONING	quantifying things and logically proving them
MUSICAL	discerning, pitch, rhythm, sound, tone, etc.
ENVIRONMENTAL OR NATURE	understanding nature and other living things
SPATIAL OR ARTISTIC	visualization of the world in 3D

"It wasn't like we just stepped off the street and said 'We want to do something.'

We were well trained."

- REV. C.T. VIVIAN

find yourself in a harder spot. It is not the only tool in your toolbox however, it is a good one to have on hand if you should need it.

You need to be educated. It doesn't matter how you learn, just learn. You can take formal routes, as I have, like attending institutions and obtaining certificates, degrees, and licenses. Other options are to learn in more informal ways, like Shockey. Both formal and informal education are important but if nothing else please focus on doing at least one. Regardless, keep in mind that learning through experience can sometimes be a really lengthy process. Shockey wasn't allergic to going to conferences to learn more about printing and he regularly was learning bits and pieces from vendors who would frequent the production plant. However, he also worked in that production plant for 30 years[25] to know all that he knew about printing.

I fundamentally believe that everyone is smart in at least some way. But it is not just about being smart or about knowing. It is about using all the smarts you have and doing what you know. At the time this book was written, approximately 34% U.S. population was degreed yet its citizens still aren't as impressed with informal education as much as formal education. However, that perception is changing and because of that change I do have one caution, "informally educated" must not be confused with dumb and untrained. As a holy, educated, motherf*cker it is my hope that whatever you choose, avoid choosing to be dumb and untrained. Perhaps it is a blindspot I possess but I cannot think of any way a dumb and untrained person can work their way out of an unthinkable tragedy except on a hope and a prayer. While I believe fervently in the power of prayer, I want you to couple prayer with a strategy. Hope is not a strategy.

---

[25] Jesus only lived to be 33 years old. Just saying!

68

chapter four

MOTHERF*CKER

MOTH · ER · F*CK · ER

/ ˈməTHər ˌfəkər /

noun

a person or thing of a specified kind,
especially one that is formidable,
remarkable, or impressive in some way

Motherf*cker? I had a really hard time with the term. My biggest issue was the literal term – person who has sex with their mother. How traumatic! Traumatic but a real occurrence for many of my ancestors who withstood the abominations associated with legalized, institutional slavery across the globe. A larger problem related to term use is that we don't bother ourselves with understanding the historical significance of the words we use. Many people are unaware of the true horrors of chattel slavery here in the United States of America and its' connection to words like motherf*cker. During that time, if Black men were deemed to be bucks, they were implored to have sex with innumerable women, some they knew and some they did not in order to produce more "property." It is highly possible that men were forcibly required to have sex with their own sisters, daughters, cousins, aunts, and yes, even their mothers. While history books vary in the recounting of these events and some historians claim that the practice is unfounded, I still believe it occurred. Through oration, these stories have withstood the historical whitewashing of US history. Besides, why wouldn't I believe that this barbaric practice occurred? The horrors of chattel slavery seemed to have no bottom. Why would this particular act be beneath that moral code of slave owners? That assessment alone should be reason enough for me not to use the term motherf*cker.

Now consider the incongruence between using a term like motherf*cker and the holy, educated parts of me. Well, you also have to consider that I have been cursing since I was in elementary school. Cursing was my vice as a kid. When I prayed to God to forgive me of my sins, I was so young that I didn't really hold much in my brain as a sin except for my little potty mouth. But that didn't keep me from cursing. In fact, this approach to sin can sometimes be one of the unfortunate teachings of some Christian leaders. While they don't believe that you can do anything good enough to get into heaven, they also believe that you can't do anything bad enough to keep you out.

My all-time favorite pastor is Reverend Adam Hamilton because he is a scholar - preacher and his thinking reminds me of Uncle Sam the Sunday school teacher. Pastor Adam dissected Jesus's Sermon on the Mount and I was inspired by two critical points he made. In the Sermon on the Mount, Jesus makes a couple of statements that are interesting. One focal point was that Christians are expected to seek perfection. It is a high bar and wouldn't we all be better if that were our aim? Another focal point in that same sermon is that all people have sinned and come short of God's glory. Unfortunately, the theology is sometimes interpreted that Jesus is the only way into heaven so when you do something bad, confess and Jesus's blood pays it all—including your irrevocable admission ticket. Pastor Adam shared how this represents a low bar in Jesus's sermon that often Christians barely try to clear. I was no different in my beliefs for an extended period in my life.

Consequently, while still in grammar school I would ask for forgiveness and keep cussing. It's not because I value cursing necessarily. Rather, I value humor. In fact, I would place humor in my top three values and I observed early in life that people laugh when I curse. It's kind of weird. When other people curse, I notice that observers may get scared, worried or put off. Me? When I curse, people find it to be hilarious. And while I value making people laugh, what about the holy and educated parts of

71

me. Holy people don't curse (at least publicly) and educated people don't curse either. I hear it's an indication of a limited vocabulary. Therefore, using motherf*cker is truly incongruent, right?

I struggle with all of it and, as I said in the opening, I didn't choose the name. The name was given to me and it's an accurate, although an uncouth, description. I am a holy, educated motherf*cker. Believe it or not, God invited me to embrace the title[26]. In general I am a brave person, but not courageous enough to use such a harsh word on the cover of a book without divine intervention. While my parents and grandparents are deceased, my aunties and uncles are still alive. My personal preacher will see and read this work. My clients will find out that I've written this, too. In fact, it took me two years to accept my title enough to even type the three words out. Once I did, my holy purposeful work became more and more obvious to me. To be clear, God did not give me the title, God invited me to accept the title. As such, I will do my best to honor all the other ways in which the term motherf*cker is used in hopes that in doing so I can be fully authentic about all that is necessary to overcome the unthinkable—including the uncouth parts.

My language is cultural not remedial.

- REVEREND KIMBERLY JONES

[26] Don't try to debate me on this. If I believe God is instructing me, there is nothing you can say or do to change my opinion.

In alignment with my general approach to any work I do, I decided to dig into the definition of motherf*cker a little deeper. There are several uses and they all mean slightly different things. This is not an exhaustive list and even if it were, word-use changes constantly. Nonetheless, these are some of the ways that motherf*cker is used in the positive to celebrate or salute a person:

```
You a bad motherf*cker.
```
You are an incredibly attractive person.

```
You are a bad motherf*cker.
```
You're a courageous person.

```
You're bad than a motherf*cker.
```
You are a person who knows how to carry yourself while maintaining respect and someone who is looked up to by your peers.

The problem with linguistics is that, especially in the English language, words mean lots of different things to lots of different people. Also similar to the tonal languages, the tone in which you say certain words or phrases can completely change the meaning. As I've said previously, when I've been called a holy, educated motherf*cker I'm pretty certain that the person who was brandishing that term wasn't wielding it as a term of endearment. Instead I know what they really meant was, "you think you are better than us and so go on somewhere with your little holy and educated mother*cking self[27]".

BAD MOTHERF*CKERS

Bad motherf*ckers. The ones who people consider to be on the fringes of society, the misfits, we are the ones who change the world. You see, a common person, a regular person who thinks like everyone else and travels the path well-traveled, doesn't do revolutionary things. You can't be singled out if you don't stand

[27] In that instance motherf*cker was used as a term of emphasis.

out. So we blend. We take to being average at best, and subpar at worst, in order to fit in. Let me tell you something: subpar is not holy and it usually isn't a well thought out educated plan either. When I consider all that we, our physical bodies, can do involuntarily, I am hard pressed to believe that we are not intended for great things when we put forth conscious, concerted effort to allow our difference to be our superpower.

To create the new and different we need people who keep tugging at the heartstrings of what we deem to be acceptable and see something bigger and better. Those of us who encourage others to lean in to whatever it is that makes them better, brighter, and different, we are the motherf*ckers. I have fought this reality in my own life. It has been others who have invited me to encourage the left out and the left behind – to lift people up.

To be that motherf*cker.

Once I delivered a keynote entitled, Unity Not Uniformity: Lessons from the Holy, Educated Motherf*cker. The content hinged on this idea that some people are holy, and they irritate the educated and the motherf*ckers. In the keynote I also suggested that other people are educated and they frustrate holy people with their facts and figures because faith isn't factual. But educated people also tend to upset the motherf*ckers in the world because motherf*ckers want to blow up the system if it isn't working even if that isn't the smartest and most prudent thing to do. One additional point of the keynote was that motherf*ckers upset everybody because they just don't seem to care about the feelings of others if those feelings get in the way of progress. The overarching idea, was that we need holy people, educated people, and people who are motherf*ckers. I felt I was uniquely qualified to deliver this content, because like a few people in the world, I am all three.

The conference was full of Black people. In fact, it was the All Black National Convention. I was nervous and, for the record,

I am never nervous to speak[28] but it was a Sunday morning in Houston. I thought to myself that certainly on a Sunday morning, in Texas, in a crowd full of Black people, there are going to be a lot of holy people there. This conference was marketed to people who had started their own successful businesses as well. Indeed there were going to be a lot of educated people there too, right? Could I stand in front of hundreds and call myself a holy, educated motherf*cker when holy, educated people don't curse? Can I, in a group of holy and educated people, use these terms?

The person who introduced me was masterful. He listed many of my business credentials and academic pursuits, then he said, "Get ready to hear lessons from the holy, educated motherf*cker." The paradox of it was jarring and perfect. And to my surprise, the crowd roared. They loved it. Why? Because the world needs a little edge and the world is not all that excited about vanilla; we look for people who are a tad unorthodox and unique to inspire us at times. We look to those who have overcome and have risen to different heights. To my surprise, my most fervent fan that day was a pastor of a Christian church from Arkansas. He encouraged me and said that the message was clear even if the language was uncouth. One thing he was certain of was that almost all of his church members had heard the term motherf*cker, if not used it, before. He invited me to his church to speak and asked that I use "MFer" instead of motherf*cker. To which I replied, "Well, of course!" as I thought that was more than appropriate.

The bad motherf*cker is courageous. Even in the face of fear, the bad motherf*cker takes a stand anyway. The rest of that shit? Throw it in the trash. Lack of self-discipline? Throw it in the trash. The inability to embrace who you are? Throw it in the trash! Living a lie to make others more comfortable? Throw it in the trash. Excluding people on the basis of things they cannot control? Throw it all in the trash. Poverty? Hunger? Child abuse? Domestic abuse?

[28] Typically the larger the crowd the more at ease my nerves.

Throw it in the trash. Unthinkable challenge? The bad motherf*cker believes that she can overcome it. All the ills of the world are things that the bad motherf*cker observes and says, "I can change that."

The people who understand that doing something to change things is better than begrudgingly, blindly allowing things to stay broken. The people who help us move these needles are the motherf*ckers of the world who will take the risk. In that regard, count me among the bad motherf*ckers. But as you do so, know that I am not only an outlier or unique individual who is out here flying my freak flag[29] in an unconventional way in order to challenge the parts of solidified systems that are no longer working for us. When faced with overcoming the unthinkable, sometimes you have to be a bad motherf*cker. I am a bad motherf*cker in lots of beautiful ways but I am also a bad motherf*cker in ways that are less than admirable.

THIS MOTHERF*CKA!

This motherf*cka!

You are a person who has done something astonishing and wrong.

As people embark on their life's journey it is tempting to think that they and others have been pillars of excellence and ethical behavior their entire lives. As an executive coach, I know better. And having spent my life in the church listening to people testify in public, confess sins in private, and pray for themselves and

---

[29] Joe Gerstandt highlighted the importance of the "freak flag."

others, I know that everybody has something that they don't feel great about lurking in their past (sometimes in their present). For example, it is a precarious notion that one in four women have been raped but no one professes to know, to have known, or to have been a rapist. What's even more interesting is how shocked people act when they hear about horrors of rape or sexual abuse. Do you remember the show To Catch a Predator? There were so many unassuming people stealthily working to have sex with little kids.

As a different example, people will profess to abhor stealing but you want to know how many dependents miraculously disappeared when the Internal Revenue Service started to require social security number identification? Seven million! That number represented a 10% reduction in tax dodging from the prior year when taxpayers only had to provide the names for children they were claiming as exemptions. That means at least one in every ten people is willing to completely fabricate a whole kid to get out of paying their fair share of taxes. Before you roll your eyes at a meager 10%, you should understand that the resulting revenue for the Treasury was $2.8 billion dollars in taxes.

It sucks when you find these things out about people you know personally or when you learn it about your heroes. One of my heroes is the[30] Rev. Dr. Martin Luther King, Jr. When Dr. Michael Eric Dyson wrote a book about King, I recall being offended. I May Not Get There With You: The True Martin Luther King, Jr. shared all the gutter behavior of King. In the book, Dyson was making an attempt to show his readers that if King, a man with flaws, could do so much then so could they. Before that book, I had a pretty angelic view of King. In 1966, King had only a 33% favorable rating. By the time I was reciting his I Have a Dream speech in 6th grade, his approval rating was over 90%. The numbers from the Gallup poll were based on a false sense of who he was as a man and not rooted in the reality of what he actually believed or who he really

---

[30] The "the" is added for emphasis on his importance to me. I made the editor leave it.

was in either case. Like many Americans, I was in love with the image of King, not the holey King. The truth is that Dyson's work and impact should have inspired me more at the time. Instead, in 2001, I got mad with Dyson for having the audacity to disparage King. My visceral reaction may have been fueled by the fact that I had ordered the book exactly one day before I knew my financial life was in ruin and I could've used that cash. Afterall at $25, the hardcover version cost more than what I had left in my bank account at the time. To add insult to injury, my desire for decorum was overshadowing my desire for truth. Add those two together and the result was that I was irrationally angry with Dyson for merely sharing some truths. To me, the world didn't really need to know about King the unfaithful husband. Besides, in the United States we do an awful job of showcasing the commonplace presence of Black excellence, often displaying the lowliest of the Black experience. As such, I tend to want to right that ship by overcorrecting when recounting the life of a person like King.

I am different today. Today I strive to be a lover of the truth and more like Dyson myself. Dyson understood something I did not at the time. He had lived long enough to know that all people have flaws without exception. In fact, the greatest people have some grave flaws. What you gain with additional years on the planet in an increased chance of experiencing the unthinkable. It also presents a higher probability of a gutter moment or two. While King was a young man, it is important to know that the FBI depended on the chances that King was just as human as the rest of us and used information about his infidelity to discredit and to try to control him. A long life is not guaranteed to make you wise but it is guaranteed to render you at mercy of a trying, unthinkable situation that requires a little grit, resilience or Finnish sisu[31] for you to make it through victorious.

[31] Sisu doesn't fully translate in English but the concept loosely means stoic determination.

I understand now more than ever what my paternal grandmother meant by, "keep living baby." She passed away when I was still in college which, of course, was before the dreaded 1374. I needed to live just a little longer to have a truly unthinkable moment. I also needed to live just a wee bit longer to see that I, too, can hurt another person causing an unthinkable situation for them. Sometimes I have done so without intention and other times, it was absolutely intentional. Life and living will teach you that you need some kind of belief system, you need some know-how, and you need this thing that you probably don't have to use that often—a little motherf*cker gene.

When I woke up one day with very little money I had some choices to make. Some were short term choices and others were longer term choices. For example, I immediately tightened my budget. Everywhere I could, I cut costs. For birthdays and Christmas, I didn't buy my kid one thing. After all, he was a very spoiled grandson who didn't even seem to know the difference when he was opening far too many gifts from his grandparents, aunts, and uncles. I canceled all trips unless someone else was footing the bill. I also figured out a way to eat lunch every day for less than $5.00. Most days I could eat lunch for less than $2.50 at a time when the average cost of lunch was at about $8 with the company subsidy. For dinner, I would take my son to various happy hours because the two of us could have an entire meal at the likes of McCormick and Schmicks for less than $10 total. I started consistently participating in a carpool which is really hard for a person who is commuting 80 miles roundtrip each day and has a kid in daycare but I did it. For about two years I didn't buy one book. I didn't purchase any music. I didn't go to any movies if I had to pay. I completely battened down the hatches and prepared for this difficult crisis ahead. In fact at one point, I asked my mother if my son and I could move in with her so that I could save the money I was allocating for the mortgage. She said no, which is still hilarious to me[32], but she helped with daycare expenses. My then in-laws got my mortgage back in good standing and I sold my college car to a family member. But none of that was

79

how I completely got out of more than $60,000 worth of debt.

Doing all of those things for almost two years, I was still a little over $35,000 in the hole in addition to normal household expenses like having a mortgage and a car note. I was in a numb state of sadness. Every day I walked through the world looking and acting like the bubbly person I always had been, but I was at my wits end. Today, I know that my debt elimination strategy was too aggressive. I probably should have had a longer timeline so that I didn't eliminate all entertainment but back then, I just couldn't stand the idea of being in that kind of debt. I had grown up in an environment whereby we were in poverty but we didn't owe people. We were just broke and to me there was a difference.

During my own Operation 1374, I started dating[33] one of my childhood friends. Growing up I had always admired him. He was a few years older and I was smitten. I wasn't enamored because of what he said, he never said much to me. The closest I got to him was sitting across the table in Uncle Sam's young adult Sunday School class. I was head over heels based solely on his charisma at a distance and a few phone calls that I'm sure my mother was monitoring. When he graduated high school, I didn't see him at all, but we randomly connected during this time, and we were both adults so we went out on a few dates. He was as charismatic as I remembered and he knew all of my family so I presume he knew my situation too. Folks can't keep your secrets and why would they? For the first time ever, they had something to dangle over the head of the little holy, educated, motherf*cker. I was still married and my divorce from my first husband was not close to being final. By definition, I was being an infidel but that wasn't the worst of my actions.

---

[32] Some of the others had moved back home a time or two but I'm not bitter.

[33] It took several iterations of this section before I could muster the desire to use the word "dating."

I can honestly say that I got into that relationship with my childhood friend thinking that he was a regular guy, going to work every day just like I did. He was driving a beat up pickup truck and I visited him at work several times so I had no reason to think anything different. Maybe it's that I didn't want to see anything differently. I don't know but I did run a background check and it came back with nothing[34]. Regardless, somewhere around six months of dating, there was a pivotal moment that changed everything. This singular incident made it clear to me that he was engaged in illegal activity. It was merely one data point but an impactful one that caused me to question how I had missed all the other signs. It was a moment that if you had asked me before it happened to me, I would have thought there was no way I would put up with those behaviors from a man. I would have emphatically insisted that I would break things off immediately with anyone who acted as he did.

The first data point was that his home was far more expensive than he should have been able to afford based on the quick math I was doing in my head about his estimated salary at the time. But then, I was able to have a home like that. I was just cheap, and then there's the 1374 fiasco. So his house alone wasn't a red flag, just a pink one so I overlooked that point. Another data point stemmed from the time we took a trip to Los Angeles. We were at the mall and he didn't seem to flinch when I was admiring a Louis Vuitton bag. Instead, he asked me if I wanted it and when I said that I loved it but that it was too expensive, he bought it outright with cash. Ignore the fact that people in my wealth category at the time weren't dropping a couple thousand dollars on a handbag in the early 2000s. I told myself that perhaps just the people I knew weren't spending their money in that way. Afterall, he couldn't possibly have a car note on that old beat up truck so maybe this was how he was frivolous with his money. And remember that I moved in cash as well, so again, by itself,

---

[34] Listen! I had just gotten taken for everything I had. A background check was in order.

81

this handbag purchase wasn't a red flag. It was another pink flag.

Later that evening, he left me at the hotel and I didn't see him again until it was time to leave for the airport. When I awakened, my stuff was pretty much packed. To this day I don't really unpack my bags when on trips and I was no different back then. So I didn't need to go through my luggage in detail. I simply tossed my toiletry bag in my Louis Vuitton tote and was ready to get back home. My son was with his paternal grandparents in North Carolina so there was no motherly rush to get back home but I was itching to return to Kansas City. This environmentalist, Rick, and I were staging a coup at the production plant and had a tree-hugging master plan going on that I did not want to miss. In all, I was in a good mood and I was simply excited to get back to work. I had gotten to take a trip to California having never been there before and he had spoiled me with gifts. He was in a good mood, too. I think it was because he was expecting me to be mad about him not coming back to the hotel but I wasn't. I generally sleep soundly so I didn't even know until morning that he hadn't been there all night. In general I try not to be retroactively angry about things so I was cool. In his relief, he grabbed my bag and we headed to the airport. When we got to the security gate at LAX, I got stopped by TSA. When they opened and started inspecting my luggage, I was surprised. There were several things in my luggage that I did not recognize. There were several pairs of shoes with really thick heels and other feminine looking containers but I had never seen them before. Interestingly, my bag had a really strong chemical odor. I knew this was my bag though because the other stuff in there was clearly mine. Curiously, my travel partner didn't stop and wait when I got stopped. In fact, a casual observer would have thought that we weren't even together. He moseyed on through security leaving me there alone for the search. The TSA security guard didn't seem to be alarmed by the overwhelming smell of chemicals coming from my bag. Perhaps I recognized the smell from working in a printing facility for so long. What I do know is that for reasons I still do not understand, they put everything back inside my luggage and let me go through. It could be that they thought it was fingernail polish remover or some other over-the-counter, fairly benign chemical. I truly don't know but when I got on the plane I tried to question my travel partner about why he left me, the unfamiliar items in my luggage, and the smell. Like the flip of a switch his eyes looked like monster's eyes and he instructed me not to ask him any questions. It was a long, silent flight home.

Unknowingly or not, I'm pretty sure that day that I was trafficking drugs. I never got an answer and when we landed in Kansas City I also never saw those items again. There are women who have served decades of time in jail for similar actions and because the war of drugs was still in full effect, I imagine no one would have believed my claims of ignorance. Furthermore, wealth, not culpability, determines outcomes[35] in the criminal justice system and prior to 1374, I didn't have the kind of money necessary to pay for competent counsel if I got stuck with a felony drug charge so I certainly didn't have it afterwards.

When I returned safely to my house with this useless, expensive ass Louis Vuitton bag, I started looking around for confirmation of what I already knew. You see I had grown up in the middle of Kansas City during the height of the crack cocaine epidemic. My neighborhood was reminiscent of the movie New Jack City when I was in middle school. What I saw and encountered on my way to school every day was the stuff of network television afterschool specials and independent documentaries. Let the statistics tell it, my life should look very different right now because I had to frequently navigate land mines full of drug activity and sketchy personalities. All around my childhood home there were drug houses. There was one next door and one next to that. There were absolutely two across the street. So our house was right in the middle of the chaos associated with a drug block. Police patrolled the area all day driving down the street at least 20 times in a single day. Sometimes they would stop and frisk everyone but most of the time, they just drove down the street policing

---

[35] Just Mercy by Bryan Stevenson provides a detailed account of the data.

what was happening. With all that attention, they still weren't there when some lady suffering from addiction to crack cocaine would leave her baby as a deposit for drugs. The police happened to miss all the times when people would come through from the surrounding suburbs to feed their habits. They were never there when there was a driveby shooting. And they certainly didn't seem to be there when I was studying late and the people on the street hustling were violating the noise ordinance. Want to know when they were there? Well, they were there after someone had been murdered, beaten, or raped. They were miraculously there when there were large amounts of money moving through that they could confiscate. They were also there one day when I didn't feel like walking to the library to study but this time they were still not there to protect and to serve, but again to police.

This fairly quiet day, I was sitting at the dining room table working on an AP History paper for Mr. Gene Blair's class. Our house had a ton of visitors because there were lots of us by now as all of my older siblings had gifted me with several nieces and nephews. My siblings, their spouses, and my nieces and nephews came to visit my mama every day[36]. This day my mother had left to run an errand and my oldest sister was there with me all day because she was visiting with my newborn nephew. It was quiet study when I heard this loud bam coming from the other side of our unlocked door. Then there were two more of the loud sounds when before I had any time to react, the whole door frame crashed inside. The Drug Enforcement Agency was in my house. Men were yelling with guns pointed at my head while tossing me and my sister on the floor, leaving her newborn on the couch. My mother returned fairly quickly but wasn't allowed to come in. The agents brought in the canine unit but even before this act of showmanship, you could tell from the looks on their faces that every single agent knew they had made a mistake. I could decipher it immediately. Perhaps it was the number of religious books they saw all around,

---

[36] This number represented 20 visitors if no church members or neighbors stopped by.

84

or maybe it was the impeccable nature of the furniture, or my study materials on the dining room table. Whatever it was, it was glaringly obvious that they knew they weren't inside a drug house.

Two hours later, I was allowed to get up from the floor. The dogs had successfully found a bag of potpourri and the agents were about done with their paperwork. When I was allowed to go upstairs to my bedroom, there were two officers in the tiny space—my tiny space. One seemed to be admiring all the certificates of academic accomplishment on my dresser and the other was reading my journal. They looked shocked when I walked into my own room. I was livid.

But I said nothing[37].

Of all the terrorism we were experiencing on the streets, this was how these public servants were spending their time—violating my private space. To make matters worse, I had a test the next day and my paper wasn't even close to being done. For all that inconvenience, all I overheard the agents say to my mother was, "We are sorry ma'am" and that was it. There was no restitution paid for any of it and my mother had to pay to fix our door herself which they could have just opened instead of pulverizing with a battering ram.

My familiarity with this level of disruption had previously served as a negative hole in my experiences in my mind. Prior to the TSA search at the airport, I had always looked back on it with a twinge of embarrassment. Although my childhood home wasn't a drug house, as a youth I learned all about drug activity and drug busts from just sitting outside sometimes and watching. Who could have known that in the future it would actually serve as a form of edumacation.

---

[37] To me it is sad that even when violated, I had learned not to challenge police.

85

How else would I have known to behave with a sense of neutrality when I noticed the unfamiliar items in bags at the airport? It was instinctual from years of casual levels of harassment from police. I had also picked up some residual knowledge about how drugs, drug paraphernalia, and drug money were moved and stored.

This information was helpful to me when I was back at home in Kansas City but still reeling from the events that happened in LA. When I started looking around, I knew exactly the places to look to see if Ben[38] had stored any money or material at my house. Nonetheless, my heart was hoping I wouldn't find anything. I was hoping I wouldn't find anything because I had managed to "make it out" without being involved in any kind of drug activity or even associations up to this point and that was a small miracle. But I did find something—thousands of dollars in $100 bills. It was $100,000 to be exact, neatly packaged and stored in the back of the warming compartment in my oven.

You would think that would be enough horror but that wasn't the end of it. There was something else about this guy. He was a womanizer. As well as being a womanizer, he was a disrespectful womanizer. In addition to taking me on a trip and leaving me all night long, there were a couple times when I was at his job and another woman would be there for him at the same time. One night, after the Los Angeles ordeal, with my child sleeping in the other room, my phone rang.

Woman on the other end: *Is this Nicole?*

Me: *Yes.*

Her: *I'm with Ben and he says you're not his girlfriend but I seen[39] your phone number on his phone a lot. He told me to call you so that you could clear it up and say what's what.*

---

[38] We will call him "Ben."

[39] It shouldn't matter but her poor grammar did make it worse for me.

Me: *Really? Well, he's not my boyfriend. *thinking to myself well he's not especially if he's there with you**

Her: *Thank you so much I appreciate it because I love him so much and I don't wanna waste my time if he's seeing someone else.*

Me: *Sure! No problem. May I talk to him please?*

Him: *Sounding like he's my best friend* *Hey girl! How are you doing?*

Me: *I'm fine now. Just want to make sure you and me are not together, right? And that you don't have anything here at my house either, right?*

Him: *Yeah. Yeah. That's right.*

Me: *Ok. Have a nice life.*

That was it! I had had all I could take. I called my then father-in-law and told him that I had sold my car for more than $10,000. I had actually sold it for half that amount. In the calmest demeanor, I lied and said that I couldn't claim the $10,000 sale because the purchaser didn't have the money to pay the property tax on the actual amount and emphasized that he should say he gave me the rest if interrogated by anyone. He asked no questions and just said, "Ok, daughter." Then I immediately took the one hundred thousand dollars in cash over to a friend's house and asked him and his wife to hold it until the morning. That morning I took $28,000 and I went to the bank, paying off all of my debts. This was a different stage of Operation 1374. This is the part when I began to realize what money and personal brand image can really do for a person or family. Money and image certainly ain't everything but they can make lots of things more tolerable. I walked into the bank in my engineering outfit—polo shirt and khaki pants. I had my company badge dangling from my hip, opened my Louis Vuitton tote with $28,000 in it and specified how many certified

87

checks I needed. When the bank officer asked about where the money came from, I could tell that he wasn't asking because he thought I stole it or that I was engaged in illegal activity, so with zero hint of African American Urban Vernacular I calmly said that it was from the sale of my car and from my father-in-law. He filled out the IRS Form 8300, gave me my cashiers checks, I walked smoothly out of the bank without issue, and headed across the street to the Post Office to mail my payments. Now I'm officially a bonafide liar who is spending illegal cash that isn't even mine.

When I returned home that evening, Ben was there and was keenly interested in where his money was. I told him I didn't have it. What was he going to do, call the police? He couldn't. What was he going to say to them? "This girl who works for a reputable company as an engineer stole my one hundred thousand dollars in cash that I cannot tell you the origins of but she needs to give it back." Yeah. Where was his proof? My criminal record probably included one speeding ticket and I owned a little brick house with two oak trees in the front yard. Implicit bias is a powerful thing. He wasn't calling the police. They wouldn't believe him. And if he did anything to me, all evidence would point back to him. After all, I had told my friend and his wife the entire story.

MOTHERF*CKA PLEASE!

Motherf*cker please.

You are a ridiculous person.

I could not believe him and looking back at it, I can't believe me either. That was such a dangerous move but I was in such a low place at that time. I felt like I had worked so hard. I believed that I had made so many good decisions. I believed that I had played by the rules and I had won. And here was this guy operating from no moral code and he had $100,000 cash at my house. There was no telling how much money he had stashed at other places. I was beating myself up. Asking how could I be so stupid in the 1374 instance and how could I be so gullible now. How did I not see this guy I had known my whole life for the monster he could be? How could I be so ridiculous?

He did not call the police. Surprise! But he did call my mother. Interestingly, he wasn't asking her about the money, though. He was asking her to get me to talk to him again. That's how you know that I didn't have all of his money. If I did, he wouldn't be talking with mother about anything else but getting his money back. My mama did find out about the money though and she asked my brothers to talk to me about returning it. When my brothers did mention it to me they sounded like they were worried sick that Ben would kill me. After all, we all knew people who had gotten killed for much smaller dollar amounts. I did not care about him but at my brother's urging, I gave him $72,000 back[40] but felt like I had to keep talking to him because there was no way for me to get the $28,000 returned. It was gone. Although I was bold, I did not feel strong. Instead, I felt like such a coward. Could I, for money, keep engaging with someone, who had done so much damage? Could I be that greedy? I felt cheap.

I went to my friend, the one who held the money overnight, and I said simply, "I have a son I need to feed. This guy is disrespectful to me, I know he's engaged in illegal activity, and I know he can be a monster." I did not finish my thought. I just sat there in an uncanny silence which, you should know by now, is unlike me. My friend in the most understanding way possible looked me in my eyes and said, "I understand." By now, he had watched me try to make a dollar out of $0.15 for years. He was there when I was borrowing and returning money to my mama. He was there

---

[40] My friend and his wife still can't believe they didn't borrow at least a couple hundred dollars as a holding fee.

"I wrote about my experiences because I thought too many people tell young folks, '*I never did anything wrong. Who, Moi? – never I! I have no skeletons in my closet. In fact, I have no closet.*' They lie like that and then young people find themselves in situations and they think, '*Damn I must be a pretty bad guy. My mom or dad never did anything wrong.*' They can't forgive themselves and go on with their lives."

- MAYA ANGELOU

as I was fielding phone calls sometimes regarding debts. Once when the fairly new car I was using for our carpool needed a transmission and it almost broke my spirit, he was there. He saw almost all of it. So with my friend's blessing of understanding, I spent the next eight weeks (two full pay periods) "dating" Ben.

To make amends with me, he gave me his debit card to use if I needed incidentals. I used the card for basics like gas, toiletries, haircuts, food, and daycare, etc. But also every Friday, I went to the bank and withdrew $1,000 cash. He didn't even notice. In some ways I don't see how that's anything but continuing to sleep with someone for money. I have had married friends condemn my behavior during this period. What I find interesting is that more than half of them have physically stayed in a marriage for financial reasons when all other forms of connection were gone. I don't personally see how that is any different. Them aside, I did not love him or like him and I was engaged in a physical relationship with him while accepting his money. What is that if it is not sex work? And that was my life for two months. Then I received a call at work:

Me : *This is Nicole. How can I help you?*

Different woman on the other end[41]: *Hi Nicole?*

Me : *Yes.*

Her : *I know you through Ben and he says you're not his girlfriend but I....*

Me : **Cutting her off abruptly* Listen! You and Ben need to lose my motherf*cking phone number. *Hangs up**

Motherf*cka please! If he was anything, he was consistent in his ridiculousness. That was it for real this time. I blocked his

---

[41] I saw her and the other woman later that year. They were both pregnant.

91

number, threatened him with a restraining order, and ignored all of my mother's attempts to get me to talk to him again. Afterall, she really liked this dude but she had no idea what I was dealing with. All she saw was the little boy she'd seen grow up and the amazing gifts he was showering me with. I'm sure she was confused about why I wouldn't even entertain her in conversation about it. In fact, I was borderline disrespectful to her when I would ignore her side remarks and innuendos about him.

As ridiculous as the whole thing was, I was completely out of debt and had no consistent ties to Ben from that day forward. I even had a little cash to loosen the belt a bit and return to some level of normalcy like eating lunch that didn't involve the Wendy's dollar menu. I have made peace with it all. When writing this portion of the book, I was fairly certain I would be judged harshly for this content in particular because even the lowliest people look down on sex workers. While not a fan of comparing myself to other people, one way I have been able to write this section of the book is through comparison; even Maya Angelou was a sex worker and it was her words that encouraged me to get some of my words out.

I could have gone my whole life sharing selectively the shiny parts of my journey. That choice would be inauthentic and, in essence, a lie of omission. When people meet me they feel something that makes them want to be real with me. Often they don't know what that something is and that incongruence sometimes results in distrust. That is the last thing I want. Therefore, I have taken a page out of the Political Messaging and Church Testifying 101 Handbooks—if there's a story to tell, you tell it yourself. I had effectively cleared $60,000 worth of debt and overdue payments. How? Well, honestly, because God but also because I was smart and educated. However, you cannot overlook that it is also because I was not above gutter behavior. Even I can be a real motherf*cker at times – a penny pinching, unfaithful, drug trafficking, lying, stealing, call girl-like, greedy, gangster motherf*cker.

92

Why do I tell you this story? Because in a cancel-culture people would have you to believe that anyone who has ever done anything wrong is not to be trusted. I will tell you that you have to decide if you are dealing with a person with character flaws or if you are dealing with a flawed character. Holey character flaws are inevitable. Everyone has them. You, with all your flaws, gutter moments, and unthinkable situations, are a hero to someone. You might not see it now but it will absolutely be clear once you make it out. Don't be hindered by your past mistakes or deliberate choices that didn't work out as you intended. Those things were part of your purposeful path. Besides, it is an illusion that there are perfect people. When you think that people are perfect you will be regularly disappointed.

The world's greatest men and women have something in their past that serves as a blemish on their record. My favorite is King David. Described as a man after God's own heart, this motherf*cker was a murderer. If he were still alive today he would go to jail because there is no statute of limitation for murder. Even though I believe that each of us is greater than the worst thing we have ever done, know that I checked the statute of limitations on tax evasion, drug trafficking, and theft before I wrote this chapter. I ain't trying to go to motherf*cking jail[42].

---

[42] Before you judge me too swiftly, write at least five gutter things you've done. Don't have any? Ask your best friend to write five gutter things about you.

93

chapter five

Operation 1374

un·think·a·ble

/ˌən'THiNGkəb(ə)l/

adverb

a situation or event too
unlikely or undesirable to be
considered a possibility

Some people would rather die than to be poor, broke or financially destitute. Losing wealth is often thought of as a sort of death for people. There are instances of people committing suicide because they had lost hundreds of millions of dollars. What is baffling is that in many of those cases those people still had hundreds of thousands of dollars to work with. I am not disparaging them, I am just saying that when the unthinkable happens, it is natural to pivot towards doom or to be in the dumps. It is so natural that I am not going to advise you against it. I do advise you to move as quickly as possible to the holy, educated motherf*cker parts of yourself. Your proverbial dump is not the end because there are always decision points. Losing money does not automatically mean death. Using 'no money' as the unthinkable situation, there are things that people who have ever lived in poverty know that we all can benefit from. We know that no money doesn't mean that you have to think less of yourself. We also know that if you think less of yourself, you don't have to be depressed. We know that if you are depressed, depression does not have to lead to suicidal thoughts. Furthermore, we know that having suicidal thoughts does not mean that you have to act on those thoughts. Poverty and scarcity in general teach you that you have to question your thoughts because scarcity changes the brain[43] so much that it can play tricks on you. It can make you think that nothing could be worse than your current situation.

When the unthinkable happens you don't even have to know how you are going to get out of it. Just know that it is not the end and that your ability to do these things will help you get through the unthinkable:

1. Tap into your own spiritual connection—be holy.

2. Lean on the solid places of your personality and not the holes—be wholly.

3. Draw from the whole or totality of your experiences including your education and your edumacation—be educated.

4. Be a courageous, bad motherf*cker.

5. Pull out that motherf*cker gutter behavior if need be.

I didn't lose millions but I did get taken for tens of thousands. How? I trusted someone I think I absolutely should have been able to trust. My bank account hadn't been down to these kinds of numbers in my entire adult life. Thirteen seventy four was not even in the realm of possibilities for me. It was just unthinkable.

I've had many more unthinkable moments since then. I have gotten a call at work telling me that my mother was involved in a fatal crash; killed by a drunken driver. I was fired from that executive level job I was so lucky to get even whilst being one of the top producers. I have had friends die from random conditions like pneumonia and also at their own hands via suicide. I have watched all my business dry up in two days because of a worldwide

---

[43] Scarcity: The New Science of Having Less and How It Defines Our Lives by Sendhil Mullainathan and Eldar Shafir

pandemic. As you have read in this book, I have definitely been woefully unlucky in love - loving a man who preferred my sister, being surprised by a whole baby once when I thought I was on my way to the altar, walking into a bedroom to find the man I love there with another woman and this is not the half of it. In an instant, everything can change. This is not a Nicole-specific issue. This is the human condition. I've known people who have had to deal with everything from betrayal to illness to murder. I am not unique. My story is not special. The insights from my story are special because they come from the lens of the holy, educated motherf*cker. They are not just spiritual. They are not only academic. They have come from more than just this street credibility that some of us gather from growing up in scrappy situations. These insights come from all three.

Tapping into your own holy, educated motherf*cker is essential to overcoming the unthinkable. And while you might not be a holy, educated motherf*cker, maybe you can learn something from my holy, educated motherf*cker tendencies? When you are faced with a situation, financial or otherwise, that is so unlikely that you can't even consider it a possibility, what do you do? I suggest ramping up your own Operation 1374 and use the HeMF survival guide to find your way up and onward.

The HeMF Survival Guide

HOLY

Be still, and know that I am God.
Psalm 46:10

I own that this book may not be for everyone. If you are atheist, the holy portion of this book likely won't resonate with you. Many of the gay, lesbian, queer, and transgender people I know have been deeply wounded in churches by slyly hateful people who under the auspice of religion have left them feeling as if to believe in no God is less painful than believing in a God who hates them because of their sexual orientation, sexual expression, gender assignment, etc. It pained me to think about how my friends would not resonate with the holy part of me. Stating that I believe Christians have gotten this part wrong won't help that fact. Yet, I still feel obligated to state it.

Here is my hope;

If you believe in any spiritual idea at all, you will see that part of your way onward is to pray and meditate. There is one thing for sure about talking with God[44], no one can tell your business. Pray or chant as much as you can and as often as you can. The bible states three benefits of prayer. These three are necessary in Operation 1374. One is devotional in nature. Seeking and being in the presence of God can calm one's spirit. Secondly, when you pray you petition God for what you want to be true. You are in essence speaking things into existence with your ask. Thirdly, it also never hurts to have prayer warriors interceding for you through prayer. I am convinced that sometimes I made it through because righteous people were waging war through prayer on my behalf. More important than prayer, is listening to God and watching for direction from the universe through meditation.

---

[44] If the word "God" is triggering just speak out into the universe when no one else is around.

99

"Jesus Christ is the Buddha of the West."

- THICH NHAT HAHN

The practice of meditation is crucial to calming the mind when you face the unthinkable. In my opinion, Buddhist Lamas are the best at teaching the practice of meditation. I specifically engage in transcendental meditation as a daily practice to keep my mind calm all the time. The way I see it, when the unthinkable happens it is better to be in a mindful spirit than in a tumultuous spirit. If you practice organized religion, you may not get full support for learning how to meditate from a Buddhist. But trust me, meditation and yoga aren't making you less of a Christian (or Muslim, or Wiccan, or Hindu or Voodoo Priestess, etc.), they are making you a better Christian. Most importantly, meditation will keep you from losing your mind.

While I believe that God speaks to me in my dreams, I know that idea is a little far out there for people. If it resonates with you, consider reading Hearing God Through Your Dreams by Dr. Charity Virkler Kayembe, as I mentioned previously, to learn more about how to interpret your dreams for direction. I've been engaged in the practice for years and God has only given me direction about my own life. God hasn't spoken to me about what someone else should do yet. I am telling you this because the focus should always be on you. You are the only one you can control. Thinking about or trying to control other people is too much during stable times. Consequently, it is definitely too much to bear while trying to navigate the unthinkable. If dream interpretation is not your thing, don't fret. There are people I know and respect who won't even allow me to talk about the practice with them. It is ok.

Finally, consider doing "The Work" by Byron Katie. She has two worksheets that will help you get to a neutral position so that you clearly decide your path forward rather than be in reaction mode all the time. While she is a polarizing figure, I subscribe to the outcomes of her work. If you want peace about an issue, do the work. Two specific worksheets can be found on her website and are named 'Judge Your Neighbor' and 'One Belief At A Time'. The approach is theologically agnostic and helps you to question your thoughts so that you can have peace in any situation—including the unthinkable situations.

The purpose and passion sections might have seemed a bit incongruent in the Holy chapter. They were not. Remember that one definition of holy is to be dedicated or consecrated to God or a religious purpose. In the middle of the unthinkable, find ways to engage in things that are in alignment with your purpose. If you don't know your purpose, again don't fret. This survival guide is not meant to cause you additional stress. Start with thinking about these things:

1. What are some things you absolutely love to do?

2. What are some things that people regularly ask you to do that come easy to you?

3. What is one thing that you know the world needs from you and you have been sitting on it for too long?

Engaging in these types of activities will lift your spirit. Trust me on this. Try to find 80 minutes total a week where you are doing nothing but serving people in this way. It doesn't have to be big. For example, do you love sports? Find time to help a person with their form or play a pickup game with some young people. Perhaps people always ask you to help them with their writing or call you for advice. Either way, find time to focus on giving in that way. Generosity, when it's not mired in martyrdom, is proven to make you feel better. For some people it helps to serve in an area where people are in a worse situation than them. Not that you will be grateful for your unthinkable situation but it will give you greater perspective about your situation.

Your passion projects will likely align with your purpose but if not, engage in projects that bring you lots of energy. Advocating for others, rooting for your kiddos in their pursuits and more will give you nice distractions. Some people will say that you aren't dealing in reality. Now for what I don't want you to think—don't go engaging in activities that numb the brain or make your situation worse. What do I want you to think—your holy purpose and passion will guide you towards healthy indulgences.

WHOLLY

```
All things work together for the good
of them who love the Lord. Romans 8:28
```

It is hard to imagine that there is some purpose behind your pain. While I do not believe that God organizes the universe to cause you pain, I do believe that God will "bestow upon you a crown of beauty for your ashes." When your whole world feels like it has come crashing down in a pile of burnt ashes, know that there will be a beautiful crown about you in the end. Perhaps you will be stronger. Maybe you will be more loving or compassionate. It could be that you end up in a place where you can lift the spirits of others when they experience a similar event. Trust in the idea that it all works together for your good—every experience good and bad. Pay attention to the entirety of your life's experiences to help you get through this new one. Do not look at the past and wish for it to be different. Look at where you are and craft your plan for where you want to be. Allow the past to serve you by focusing on what positive things you learned or what positive attribute you gained from the totality of your experiences. You are not trying to fall in love with the pain of the past. In fact, I have adopted the personal belief that there is something really beautiful about the past—it is over. It is the learning from the pain that will serve you very well not necessarily holding on to the past in the present. Now don't decide to manufacture pain. That is wholly unnecessary. It is one thing to end up in a painful situation because of circumstances. It is another thing to seek pain because it is familiar. I am proud of what I learned from being in poverty. I am also proud of what I've learned from living on a drug block. I appreciate what I have learned about people and the compassion I've built from my experiences with personal loss. I take my learnings from failed relationships into every new partnership I embark upon. Hold onto the learnings. The pain doesn't need to come along for the ride.

HOLEY

```
Not that I have already obtained it
or have already become perfect, but
I press on so that I may lay hold of
that for which also I was laid hold of
by Christ Jesus. Philippians 3:12
```

In the middle of an unthinkable crisis, remember that you have everything you need to find your onward. It can be tempting to start to wish you were more detail oriented, more beautiful, thinner, heavier, smarter, more or less talkative, funnier, richer or poorer[45]. Stop it! Focus on your strengths. This action is more important in the gutter than it is at any other time because in stress, we have a tendency to try to lean into our weaknesses. Every time I've seen it, it's been ugly. Resist the urge.

Now about those holey experiences, be careful there, too. People will try to tell you that you need certain experiences to get out of the gutter. I'm not so sure. Do you need a degree if you are an amazing jeweler? I don't think so. There are plenty of experiences that you have not had but all the experiences you've had will serve you in astonishing ways. God would have it no other way.

If you believe God is instructing you to do your work, there should be nothing anyone can say or do to change your opinion. By its very definition, faith is a belief, not something that can be proven. Even though it cannot be proven, these strongly held beliefs inspire people to do some amazing good in the world. That's how you know in your heart it is from God. It is helpful and good. Many secular organizations buy into and use this idea. Alcoholics Anonymous begins the first step of their program by inviting people to accept and acknowledge a power greater than

---

[45] I've never met anyone who wanted to be poorer but I imagine it's a thing because of the quote "More money, more problems."

themselves. Frederick Douglas said it this way, "One man and God make a majority." A person driven by faith is unstoppable. The goodness in that is that holiness can inspire the masses. If this is you, it is your responsibility to use your connectedness to uplift, not to tear down. Stay out of the spiritual malpractice or the tearing people down lane. It is not a good look when you profess to be holy. It is the job of the holy to be the eternal optimist.

EDUCATED

The heart of the prudent getteth knowledge; and the ear of the wise seeketh knowledge. Proverbs 18:15

If you've read this far, it is likely that you think that being called educated would be the one adjective in the Holy, Educated Motherf*cker title that I could fully embrace. Well, not entirely. When Barack Obama ran for president of the United States of America, many news pundits criticized him for being educated at Harvard. He was said to be an elitist and that association made him out of touch with the common United States citizen, 66% of whom are not college educated. How could that be? He had worked as a community organizer for years and many people loved him. There were many things he was, out of touch is not something I'm sure I can rally behind. What I can rally behind is that being educated is not always applauded. After all, the term "nerd" is not meant to be a term of endearment either. I am classically educated. I have a Bachelors of Science degree in chemical engineering. I have a Masters in adult education and I have my Doctorate in leadership and management. I ain't no dummy. However, oftentimes the education signals for people a lack of practical experience. Even people I respect have said to me on several occasions, "You got books smarts but common sense ain't so common."

I could be faced with this type of vitriol by simply not knowing something that most people learn from their parents. It's a common occurrence when you are the sixth child of seven children. People forget you are even there so it makes sense that

105

they would also forget to teach you a common sense thing or two. For some things, you simply need an "ignore" button.

EDUMACATED

Regardless of if you are college educated or not, you fall into this category of the educated. What does it mean to be educated? Lived experiences are a form of education. If you have a set of lived experiences that are vast, unconventional, and or different from the norm, you learn things about the world that people with fairly basic lives miss out on. There is no price that could truly match the value of those lived experiences. They are invaluable.

There is also basic skill, talent, and ability as a form of education. Some things are not learned in books. They show up in the form of actual skills. Understand what you are dealing with. Pay attention. Also use your credentials to identify all the opportunities that are in front of you. If you are skilled but have no credentials, you know what you need to do. Either your work needs to be so good that no one cares or you need to change the state of your affairs. It is not just a piece of paper. You will learn something that will make you better. But also be sure to resist the urge to allow a piece of paper to confound you. Sometimes we studied a topic because it was convenient. If that study is no longer serving you, focus on making the shift. As an example, I earned a bonafide certificate as a hazardous materials manager once. It was hard work and costly. However, there is absolutely no reason for me to continue to cultivate that knowledge in any way. It served me during a time when I had a very specific job and now it does not. Learn to move on when necessary. That is common sense.

Speaking of common sense, lean into that doctorate you have in common sense. One important common sense tactic is that you need to lean into the community. When you are down and out and facing the unthinkable, it flies in the face of solid wisdom to fortify your individualistic character. You certainly get to define your community, but you need some peeps. Identify your very human resources that you will need to give you strength. Also lean on the unconventional things you have learned throughout your life up to this point. God has given you experiences, what did you learn from them. There's more than one way to be educated, nine ways in fact. But remember, whatever your education or edumacation.

1. When you know more, you have to do more.

2. Hard-earned lessons are still lessons if you learn from them.

3. Teach others along the way.

The Scientology course, The Way to Happiness, is worth a look if you are open to the unconventional nature of L. Ron Hubbard and the followers of his teachings[46]. It may be the first quasi religious moral code based wholly on the concept of common sense. The Scientology courses are very well done and I struggled to find a scripture to support this section. That could be because when religions were being organized, the idea that common people had something to add was ludicrous. Even Jesus was disparaged for being a commoner. Regardless, I have personally taken at least four courses from the Church of Scientology and they have been incredibly useful in a practical way. Get the message and try not to get caught up in the messengers.

MOTHERF*CKER

It will take the unwonted in order to overcome the unthinkable. The motherf*cker definition I claim the most and the one I most apply comes from the online urban dictionary. It has come to mean "a formidable or inexorable force." Now that's what I'm talking about.

Force is the strength possessed by a living being. It has no positive or negative charge. How we choose to be a force in our

---

[46] They are kind of like the Sweet Daddy Grace people without the great singing and good food.

107

"The most beautiful people we have known are those who have known defeat, known suffering, known struggle, known loss, [*known the unthinkable*], and have found their way out of the depths. These [*holy, educated motherf*ckers*] have an appreciation, a sensitivity, and an understanding of life that fills them with compassion, gentleness, and a deep loving concern."

- ELISABETH KÜBLER-ROSS

own lives and in the world is a decision each individual has to make. We all have the ability and the responsibility to make that choice, and if you try to opt out, to beat the system by not choosing, guess what? Not choosing is still a choice. So choose even if you have to draw out of a hat. Why? Because by not choosing, we decide to be passive participants in our own lives. We forfeit the opportunity to experience our lowest lows and our highest highs because we refuse to give of ourselves and invest in ourselves fully. That fullness is where the power lies.

It's understandable, though. We've been fed very conflicting messages about power. On the one hand, we're told that our greatest fear is that we are powerful beyond measure. On the other hand, we're told that absolute power corrupts absolutely. So maybe we're afraid that if we choose to be powerful, then corruption is inevitable. I don't know about you, but I'm not trying to be a comic book super villain. What I do want—what I want for you—is fully committed ownership of a passionate and purposeful life. It will come with some flaws.

BAD MOTHERF*CKA

```
There hath no temptation taken you
but such as is common to man: but God
is faithful, who will not suffer you
to be tempted above that ye are able;
but will with the temptation also make
a way to escape, that ye may be able
to bear it. 1 Corinthians 10:13
```

You have far more strength to overcome than you have ever imagined. If an unthinkable issue has come your way, I believe it is because you have the ability to deal with it. There is also nothing you are dealing with that someone else hasn't dealt with and know that they came out of it when some elements of their situation were much worse.

109

Otto Koning, a veteran missionary and speaker, recounts an experience that he calls, The Pineapple Story. It's a tale about when he and his wife were in Papua, New Guinea doing mission work. After struggling to find a crop that would grow in the damaged, depleted soil, the couple finally succeeded in growing pineapples. As the pineapples grew and before they ripened, they began to disappear; the people of the village were stealing them. Otto was angry about the stealing, and he was angry with himself for being angry. Finally, he decided to "give" the garden to God. Almost immediately, Otto's stress level went down; he slept better; and eventually the theft stopped. His rationale? God takes good care of God's property. I had fallen asleep watching YouTube videos and I was awakened by the pineapple story—figuratively and literally. The pineapple story was another example of letting go of the tug of war rope. How? Because if you think of it all as God's property—your skills, your money, your knowledge, your wealth, your reputations, your health, your intentions—you may find the unthinkable, in all of its' unfairness, to be more tolerable. This thought will help you untether yourself from things you don't have any longer and certainly to allow you to untether yourself from the things you cannot control. The sooner we surrender to this idea, right or wrong, the better. We worry about the past. We worry about the future. We worry about belonging and whether or not people will accept us with our flaws and missteps. We certainly worry ourselves about these things when we have negative experiences in our past. We get sad or angry about how people misunderstand, mischaracterize or misrepresent us because we are trying so hard to fit in. To surrender to the motherf*cker you are is holy. Surrender to the thoughts that serve you and direct your attention to all the things you can control and influence. Cease all efforts to lend more than general concern to those things you can do nothing about.

THIS MOTHERF*CKA

Therefore you have no excuse, O man, every one of you who judges. For in passing judgment on another you condemn yourself, because you, the judge, practice the very same things. Romans 2:1

For all that Otto Koning shared about the people of Papua, New Guinea, he left out one fact that I think is really important. They use the concept of the mokita to judge the health of their community. Mokitas are the things everyone knows but no one speaks of. The fewer mokitas, the healthier the community. We have to share and talk about our missteps so that others can live out their purpose without feeling like they have to live a lie. People ain't out here perfect. If they judge you, understand that they have that same shit in their experience. Don't allow your morality to get in the way of your breakthrough. I don't recommend that you do anything illegal. I don't have your bail money, however, you may need to do something that will make other people say, "This motherf*cka!" and you have to be ok with that. More importantly, I need you to be open to working with people who might be a little sketchy to find your way out of the unthinkable. Ultimately, I am that holy, educated, motherf*cker and with all they know about me still most people don't allow it to get in the way of the shared work we need to do together at times.

MOTHER*CKA PLEASE!

Let him who is without sin among you,
let him first cast a stone. John 8:7

My mama always said that every Jesus has a Judas. What she meant was that people who are doing good in the world will have someone who will betray and hate on them. At times, I have heard preachers disparage Judas. I take a different position which is that Judas did exactly what he was supposed to do. Given that, you can be disappointed when your Judas appears but never be surprised. Expect it. When you are on top doing amazing things, people will come for you. When you are in the gutter scraping to find your way out, people will come for you. The only time people don't come for you, well, is never. Even if you aren't doing anything at all, someone will don their Judas garb. Your work is to dig in to your best "motherf*cka please" and focus. If they haven't had your experience, let them throw their stones. You? Don't even stop long enough to get hit. You've got work to do.

There are people who think it is natural and will encourage you to grieve about your unthinkable situation. Yes and...motherf*cka please. Grieve in moments not in days or weeks or months. Try your best to live in the current moment. Of course make a longer term plan, but your survival will be tied to your ability to stay present in the moment. Try to spend as little time as possible in the past rethinking your whys. I'm not sure an after action review will help you. You will suffer more. When you have a painful thought, label that thought as a past thought, a present thought or a future thought. Then, thank the thought for coming and then work your short term plan, little steps to help you achieve the longer term goals. Change is incremental, not inconsequential. Take your small steps, they will lead to larger breakthroughs.

Your real life might be awful in the moment. Do not allow your mind to make it worse than it is. Especially don't allow the minds of other people to make your life worse than it is. You're one holy, educated motherf*cker. Now what? Get your kit together!

The subtitle of the book actually says guide[47] but I don't intend to structure or direct your steps. This is more of an arsenal of things or a kitty bag for you to pull from. In it there are tools that you may need and you can always pull them out on demand if you have them readily available as you navigate the unthinkable.

1. Ritual: Do the same thing for the first few minutes (or seconds) every morning. Do this even on the weekends. For some people this is a combination of meditation, prayer, and dream interpretation. For other people it is to wake up, stretch, and wash their face. Whatever it is, do the same thing, in the same order, every morning. You also might consider a wind-down ritual at night that includes documenting the three things you are grateful for from the day or perhaps shower with an added purpose of releasing worry.

2. Music: If you have the ability to hear and have access to music, find some music to uplift your spirit. Create a playlist. Title the playlist something fun like "Get It Together", "HeMF" or something fun that encourages you. There is only one rule, zero music that has lyrics that don't uplift the human spirit. Period. No matter how great the beat, the lyrics are what matter the most.

3. Encouragement: Find at least one person who has overcome a situation like yours or worse. The person can be someone real or imaginary, dead or alive, someone you know personally or someone you have never met. Their method may not be your method, the particulars may be different, but anything they have overcome, will serve as an inspiration for you. My person was Iyanla Vanzant in 2001. I did not know her but her book Interiors: A Black Woman's Guide to Healing in Progress was a lifesaving example of what I believed I could do.

---

[47] A Filter-Free Kit to Getting Through the Unthinkable doesn't flow off the tongue correctly.

4. Discipline: Identify one to three things that you will focus on. Be relentlessly focused on two things. First, your goal is simply to just put one foot in front of the other. Meaning, just do what absolutely is necessary for the day. Some days simple things like brushing your teeth will seem like a chore. It's ok. I've been there. In those instances know that your mind may fail you so you have to trick it. Use the Mel Robbins 5 Second Rule to help you. Count down from five and before you get to one be out of the bed walking towards the toothpaste and toothbrush.

5. Support: God sends support. Pay attention. It will be there. Open your heart. Receive it. When it shows up, accept the help. You will have friends who will only be your friends in this unthinkable moment. They will not be lifelong friends, that is ok. You will have mothers you didn't even know you had and therapists in the form of homeless men on the street. These are God's rams in the bushes[48]. Embrace them.

6. Honor: This whole book has been about honoring you—a holy, educated motherf*cker. Your way out of the unthinkable will be paved with a solid foundation of knowing who you are, not questioning who you are. Strengthen your character but don't seek to change who you are. You have work to do. There is a purpose for all of us. There is a purpose for your life and you have to believe the universe is conspiring in your favor, for me it's called faith and no one can move me from that because it has been crucial in my journey.

7. Grieve: When you feel emotions, feel them. I do have a caveat—grieve in moments. Even in grief you will have positive emotions and feelings. Feel those emotions, too. Watch children. They are skilled at this. They cry when they feel sad and smile when they feel happy. They rarely wallow in their sadness all day, all week or all month. They are quick to forgive themselves. Follow their example.

---

[48] Christian reference meaning protection that will reduce your personal level of sacrifice.

Remember, this kit is not intended to be used as a step-by-step guide to overcoming the unthinkable. Rather, it should be thought of like a toolkit that you take with you on your journey.

As I was recounting several of my stories, I thought about people who have more challenging experiences than I have had. I thought about Anthony Ray Hinton who spent decades on death row for a crime he did not commit. I thought about my friends who have gotten terminal diagnoses. I revisited the time a friend told me about her drunken father raping her. My heart cracked open as I thought about parents who have faced deportation without their children. In my reflection, I even ran through a couple scenarios I've seen on the Paternity Court TV show where people find out that their spouses have not only been unfaithful but also learn that the children they have loved their entire lives aren't their biological kids. These are simply unthinkable situations; absolutely unthinkable. These scenarios tempt me to think that I want to remove these unthinkable situations from you. I find myself wanting to relieve people, and the world really, from this kind of pain. I cannot emphasize enough how much I do not want you to suffer and of course I don't want you to have any 1374 situations. I truly don't. I resist those thoughts, however. Because it is likely that your unthinkable situation is the reason you and I have met here on the pages of this book. I believe with every fiber of my being that your path is your path to your God-work—your holy, compassionate work. Beautiful people don't just happen. Experiencing the unthinkable is part of the process of becoming an even more beautiful person than you are. Every stop, jagged edge, and crooked place along the way are all destined to help you be better; a deep, soul connected, empathetic human and as the late, great Oma Dell Price said, "Keep living baby." •

PRIVATE WORKSHOPS

If you need more information or help, reach out to me at info@nicoledprice.com to inquire about participating in or organizing the next Operation Thirteen Seventy-Four Workshop near you.

I hope to keep the cost the same $1,374per person and as always, you may bring a friend at no additional charge if you so desire. If your unthinkable situation is financial in nature, reach out to us directly for special HeMF pricing at the email above.

FOOTNOTE REFERENCES

Before you comment on the style of these references,
this is not an academic journal so I made the references
in the easiest format to understand. It's kind of like
turning gravure presses. Just go with me on this.

1. www.do-it.com hangtab website

4. Darling Nikki produced, arranged, composed,
performed and written by Prince

7. 4 Keys to Hearing God's Voice written by Dr. Mark and Dr. Patti Virkler

8. Loving What Is by Byron Katie

19. Escaping Poverty Requires Almost 20 Years With
Nearly Nothing Going Wrong by Peter Temin

29. Freak Flag Flying video by Joe Gerstandt

31. The Finnish use the word sisu to explain an unyielding resilience

35. Just Mercy by Bryan Stephenson

43. Scarcity: The New Science of Having Less and How It Defines
Our Lives by Sendhil Mullainathan and Eldar Shafir

REFERENCES BY PAGE NUMBER

6. Filter Free Fridays can be found on the social media pages @nicoledprice

13. The School for the Work organized by The Work International

15. I Know It Was the Blood written by Evelyn Simpson-Curenton

20. Purpose Driven Life by Rick Warren

20. What Color is Your Parachute

27. Myers Brigg Type Indicator created by Isabel Myers and Katharine Cook Briggs

30. Boot Scootin Boogie written by Ronnie Dunn of by Brooks & Dunn

36. The Mis-Education of the Negro by Carter G. Woodson

36. The Miseducation of Lauryn Hill by Lauryn Hill

43. Start With Why by Simon Sinek

52. All Black National Convention hosted by Dr. Boyce Watkins

54. To Catch a Predator series premiered in November 2004 on NBC

54. I May Not Get There With You by Dr. Michael Eric Dyson

55. I Have a Dream Speech by Rev. Dr. Martin Luther King, Jr.

55. Popularity of Rev. Dr. Martin Luther King, Jr. conducted by Gallup

59. New Jack City movie directed by Mario Van Peebles

72. www.thework.com Byron Katie's website

72. Hearing God Through Your Dreams by Dr. Mark Virkler and Dr. Charity Virkler Kayembe

77. The Way to Happiness by L. Ron Hubbard

78. The Pineapple Story by Otto Koning

20367351R00070